A Believer's Guide to Christian Maturity

A Believer's Guide to Christian Maturity

A. F. Ballenger

Formerly titled POWER FOR WITNESSING

3597

BETHANY HOUSE PUBLISHERS
MINNEAPOLIS, MINNESOTA 55438
A Division of Bethany Fellowship, Inc.

Originally published under the title:
Power for Witnessing

A Believer's Guide to Christian Maturity
A. F. Ballenger

This edition, 1982

Library of Congress Catalog Card Number 82-072493

ISBN 0-87123-278-2

Published by Bethany House Publishers
A Division of Bethany Fellowship, Inc.
6820 Auto Club Road, Minneapolis, Minnesota 55438
Printed in the United States of America

PREFACE

If the reader, like the Athenians of Paul's day, is searching for "some new thing" in the form of a "new doctrine," this little book will doubtless disappoint him, for it is put forth more as a teacher of diligent *doing* than as a discussion of doubtful *doctrine*.

He will have no difficulty in knowing the doctrine, who is willing to *do* the doctrine. "If any man willeth to do his will, he shall know of the teaching" (John 7:17, R.V.).

Since the book is more an exhortation to doing than an exposition of doctrine, no apology is offered for the style adopted of personally addressing the reader. The writer but describes two phases of his experience in saying that he who is ashamed of his hope will find personal work embarrassing, and will find it more to his liking to deal in "glittering generalities"; while he whose "hope maketh not ashamed" will be constrained to urge it upon others by personal appeals.

The message of the book is the Spirit's answer to the writer's heart-cries for power for Christian living and labor. And from direct contact with people in evangelistic work in nearly every state and territory in the United States, he has learned that his heart's cry was but one in a chorus of cries which will be heard from honest hearts in every land by Him whose life and lips proclaim the answer.

The only excuse for devoting so much space to "first principles" is that there is so much space for them in the experiences of the people. It makes no difference how tall or how talented men and women are, or how long they have preached or professed, if they "have need of milk and not of strong meat," *milk they must take* until they are stronger; and neither the one who ministers the milk nor the one to whom it is measured, should attempt to avoid the necessity of nursing.

It is the plan of God that ministers as well as others shall "grow in grace and the knowledge of the truth." And as one grows it is difficult to hold back that last deep soul-stirring truth, and continue to minister bottles of milk to babes in Christ. But it must be done. If it is not done, the minister with the stronger meat may find himself marveling at the multitude which follows the man who ministers the milk.

This book is for the common people. When it falls into the hands of one whose experience is broader than the book, let it be handed to some more needy soul.

CONTENTS

WHY THIS REPRINT?

A Believer's Guide to Christian Maturity was written more than sixty years ago. Its message was needed then and its message is needed today.

We are living in days when one church body after another has adopted the policies and practices of the world in order to compensate for the lack of the power of the Holy Spirit. Churches are seeking to do by organization and by large membership what God has intended to do by the power of the Holy Spirit. Madison Avenue advertising policies have been adopted. Churches, as well as other religious organizations, spend millions of dollars not only for their congregational expenses and benevolences, but also for calling attention to their activities, just as a business organization would do.

To merge is the order of the day. Lacking in power to increase the membership of the Kingdom of God, church organizations are seeking to enlarge their own membership by amalgamation. Growth in membership is not accomplished by winning more souls for the Kingdom, but rather by gathering together under one head those who already claim to be in the Kingdom. Church bodies today count their members by the millions.

Instead of Spirit-filled men at the head of these large organizations, we too often find "business-filled" men. These men have arrived at their positions largely because of their parliamentary skill and not because of the leading or power of the Holy Spirit. They know how to lead, dominate, and sway the emotions and opinions of people; consequently they rise to the top of large religious institutions.

Bigness is the predominant idea today, even with the church. It has become a big business institution.

A well-known minister, who has been greatly used in gathering pastors together for prayer for revival, once said that if the Holy Spirit were taken out of the world, ninety percent of our so-called church work would still go on and no one would know the difference! Whether he is right or wrong in his percentage, we do not know. But we have no doubt that many of the church's institutions and much of its preaching would still go on without much change.

Parallel with the trend already described is a "wild fire" movement (not an organization). Its emphasis is on supernatural power and spiritual manifestations. It is not to be confused with a genuine Pentecostal experience and its resultant gifts and power. This movement offers power without any preparation for the reception of such an enduement and ministry.

Recently in a large meeting, a man actually testified to having been baptized with the Holy Spirit several years before he was saved! Thank God we do not have too many examples as absurd as this. But we do have examples of those that testify to this experience who have no abhorrence of sin, who disclaim the necessity of separation from the world, and who neither know in experience nor even think essential, genuine day-by-day holiness of life.

There is a great vacuum today in both the world and the church; therefore many people are grasping after a deeper, supernatural Christian experience. But not knowing the Scriptures, and therefore not making a correct approach and preparation, they enter into experiences which, if not dangerous, are at least very questionable indeed. One must learn that "all is not gold that glitters," nor is all of God that is supernatural.

Between these two extremes is a genuine, biblical offer of the power of the Holy Spirit. Who will deny that we need power for Christian living and for Christian service? The baptism with the Holy Spirit is a genuine experience. It is offered to every Christian and is needed by every Christian. This experience and the resultant power is for witnessing. (Its emphasis is not on personal enjoyment, although, thank God, our true religion is a "felt" religion—there *is* personal enjoyment.) According to Christ, the baptism with the Holy Spirit is for witnessing (Acts 1:8). Jesus Christ said, "Behold, I send forth the promise of my Father upon you: but tarry ye in the city . . . until ye be clothed with power from on high" (Luke 24:49). Seven weeks later He said, "Ye shall receive power, when the Holy Spirit is come upon you: and ye shall be my witnesses both in Jerusalem, and in all Judea and Samaria, and unto the uttermost part of the earth" (Acts 1:8). Ten more days and the disciples and others (one hundred and twenty in all) received this power when they were baptized with the Holy Spirit.

This power is needed today. Our need is not for great organizations or noisy demonstrations, but rather for the power of the Holy Spirit for witnessing. We need this wonderful, heavenly Holy Spirit to witness unto Jesus Christ. We need Him to enable us to proclaim to the world that Christ died for our sins and that all who repent and believe may be forgiven and born of God.

Because of present conditions in the church today, we are constrained to publish this book, *A Believer's Guide to Christian Maturity,* which has long been out of print. The writer holds in proper balance important matters concerning this subject. He has supported his work with numerous illustrations and has clearly shown that this power is available to us by faith.

The emphasis in this book is on *doing* rather than on *doctrine*, although the reader will also find fundamental doctrine between its covers. It is a balanced presentation of this vital subject.

The author has rightly emphasized the preparation needed for this essential experience. He refers back to apostolic power in the early church, but also to apostolic preparation. At Pentecost the one hundred and twenty who were baptized and filled with the Holy Spirit were a prepared people. Therefore they were able by faith to receive the enduement of power.

The message of this book, *A Believer's Guide to Christian Maturity,* is greatly needed today.

December 1962

T. A. Hegre
Bethany Fellowship, Inc.
Minneapolis, Minnesota

CHAPTER ONE

THE PREPARATION

"But ye shall receive power, after that the Holy Ghost is come upon you; and ye shall be witnesses unto me both in Jerusalem, and in all Judea, and in Samaria, and unto the uttermost part of the earth" (Acts 1:8).

Reader, have you received this power for witnessing? If not, are you seeking this power? Have you sought, but sought in vain? Are you really anxious to receive the Holy Ghost and thereby become a powerful witness for Christ?

What do you know that you are so anxious to receive power to tell? Do you know that God through Christ forgives sins? Do you know it from personal experience? Are you prepared right now to witness to this truth in your home, in your neighbors' homes, or in the church? If not, you need *something to tell* more than power to tell it.

Multitudes of men and women are burdened with the guilt of sin. Their lives hold no hope. Many in despair are committing suicide. God wants the great sinning world to hear of His willingness to forgive, "to give unto them beauty for ashes, the oil of joy for mourning, the garment of praise for the spirit of heaviness." He wants you to witness that He does all this. Are you prepared to do it? Do you know that He does it?

A witness tells only what he knows. Do you become impatient when sorely tempted? If so, do you want power to tell this "to the uttermost part of the earth"? Are you proud, or envious, or jealous, or selfish, or ambitious, or quarrelsome, or faultfinding? Are you given to evil surmising or evil speaking? Do you love the world? Do you love worldly pleasures? Are you a slave to appetite or lust? Do you think unclean thoughts? Do you love this world's goods? Are you covetous? Are you given to jesting or foolish talking? Are you headstrong or self-willed? Jesus Christ is the power of God unto salvation from all these things. Do you know Him as such? If not, what have you to tell which makes you so anxious that God should give you power to tell it?

Don't you think that you have power enough already to publish your weaknesses to the world? If the Lord should give you the power of the Holy Ghost for witnessing while you know so little of His power to save, you would become a powerful witness against Him. Power would bring you into prominence. And just in proportion as you were brought into prominence, just in that proportion would that enslaving, besetting sin of yours be brought into prominence; and just in that same proportion would you become a powerful *false* witness, bearing testimony *against* Christ and His promise "to save to the uttermost."

The Lord gave Solomon great power when he was humble, and Solomon became a witness for God unto the uttermost parts of the earth. "And all the earth sought to Solomon, to hear his wisdom, which God had put in his heart" (I Kings 10:24). But when Solomon sinned, all the earth heard of his sin, and he became the most powerful witness in "all the earth" *against* the Lord. There were many other idolaters in Israel in the time of Solomon, but their power for evil did not compare with that of Solomon. Should the Lord baptize you with power from on high while your character is weak at any point, it would simply result in advertising that weakness to the world.

The Holy Ghost came upon the disciples on the day of Pentecost, not to persuade them to put away their self-seeking and their differences—this the Spirit had already accomplished in them. Peter did not spend the Pentecostal morning in confessing his denial of Christ, his lying, and his profanity. This work of repentance the Spirit had already accomplished in Peter. The very first thing that Peter did after the witnessing power came upon him was to begin witnessing to what he already *knew* of the power of God.

Therefore it is plain that no one can share in the "latter rain," or the fulness of the power of the Holy Ghost for witnessing, until he knows in his own life, not only that God forgives sins, but that He gives the victory over every besetting sin. Fulness of victory, then fulness of witnessing power. Something to tell, then power to tell it.

CHAPTER TWO

SOMETHING TO TELL

"What shall we do?" said the multitude on the day of Pentecost. "Repent," said Peter. If Peter had not himself repented, he could not have witnessed to the necessity of repentance. He who would be a witness that God gives forgiveness of sins and gives the Holy Ghost, must first be a witness that God gives *repentance*. If he is weak in his repentance, he will be weak in all his witnessing. For this cause many are weak and sickly among us. It is humbling to repent, and many try to escape this humbling as much as possible, not knowing that in so doing they are refusing the necessary qualifications for witnessing in power.

That the reader may be impressed with the fact that an experience necessary to witnessing to repentance must precede witnessing to both forgiveness of sins and the gift of the Holy Spirit, let the following Scripture be noted carefully:

"The God of our fathers raised up Jesus, whom ye slew and hanged on a tree. Him hath God exalted with

5

his right hand ... to *give repentance to Israel,* and forgiveness of sins. And *we are his witnesses of these things.*"

Thus the apostles declare that they are witnesses that God gives repentance. Reader, are you a witness that God gives repentance? This experience lies at the foundation of all witnessing. Are you prepared to tell in your own home, and in your neighbors' homes, and before the assembled congregation, that God gives repentance? If you are not, then the first thing to do is to repent. If you will but receive repentance and forgiveness of sins, you may receive the Holy Ghost to enable you to witness in power to what you have received. For the Holy Ghost is given to bear witness that your witness is true.

Notice the way the Scripture reads: "Him hath God exalted with his right hand ... to give repentance to Israel, and forgiveness of sins. And we are his witnesses of these things; and *so is also the Holy Ghost,* whom God hath given to them that obey him." The Lord, therefore, gives the Holy Ghost to them that obey Him, that He may unite His witness with theirs that God gives repentance and forgiveness of sins through Jesus Christ.

"Of what shall we repent? Repent of sin. What is sin? "Sin is the transgression of the law." Your repentance will be measured according to the measure of your sin, and your sin will appear exceeding sinful only as the Holy Spirit shall flash the light of the spiritual law upon your life.

"That sin by the commandment might become exceeding sinful" (Rom. 7:13). "I had not known sin, but by the law; for I had not known coveting [R.V.] except the law had said, Thou shalt not covet" (Rom. 7:7). "The law entered, that the offense might abound. But where sin abounded, grace did much more abound" (Rom. 5:20).

There will be no exceeding, abundant receiving of repentance and forgiveness of sins and of the gift of the Holy Ghost where there is not a magnifying of the law whereby sin is made to "abound" in the life and to "appear exceeding sinful."

But all this the Lord has pledged himself to do. The work of the Holy Ghost is to "convince the world of sin," and He can be depended on to do His work. The Lord through His Spirit is giving repentance. But have you received it and repented? "Only acknowledge thy transgressions"—those sins which you know to be sins—and the Lord will see to it that your repentance is complete. It is useless for the Lord to reveal additional sins while you are refusing to acknowledge and turn from those already revealed.

Some persons complain of a lack of conviction, but if they would respond to what conviction the Lord has already given, they would receive conviction of sin as fast as they were able to bear it. The Lord "lighteth every man that cometh into the world." "Walk while ye have the light, lest darkness come upon you." Walk in the light, and ye shall have fellowship one with another, and the blood of Jesus Christ cleanseth from all sin.

CHAPTER THREE

"FORGIVENESS OF SINS"

Forgiveness of sins, like repentance, is something which the Lord *gives*, and which we must *receive*. "Him hath God exalted with his right hand to be a Prince and a Saviour, for to *give* repentance to Israel, and *forgiveness of sins*."

Before anyone can receive the witnessing power from on high, he must be able to witness to the gospel truth that God forgives sins. But no one can witness to this truth unless this truth is truth in his life *at the time of witnessing*. The Holy Spirit will not furnish power to make a man's witness convincing when the fruit of the man's life gives the lie to the fruit of his lips. If the witness is not living in the knowledge and enjoyment of sins forgiven when he is trying to tell others to receive forgiveness, the Holy Ghost will not bear witness to his testimony, because the witness himself is not qualified to bear witness. And this is the reason why so many who occupy the witness stand, in the pulpit and in the pews, are so weak in their witnessing. They do not speak as those having authority, but as the scribes. If they actually witnessed to the truth, they would have to tell that they were still living under the condemnation of sin.

But why will men live under continual condemnation when the Lord is so anxious to give them forgiveness of sins?

Substantially the following conversation took place in the home of a middle-aged woman, where the writer had been invited to help her find the Lord:

Woman: I want to know that my sins are forgiven.

Minister: Have you confessed your sins?

Woman: Yes, hundreds of times.

Minister: Are you a professing Christian?

Woman: Yes, I have been a member of the church for forty years.

Minister: And never knew that your sins were forgiven?

Woman: Never.

Minister: Let us kneel down here and ask God once more to forgive, and let us pray in faith.

We knelt and prayed. Her prayer was earnest, her confession heartfelt. When we arose the conversation was continued thus:

Minister: I am glad that the Lord has forgiven your sins.

Woman: I hope He has.

Minister: But do you not *know* that He has? Have you not confessed your sins?

Woman: Yes.

Minister: And does not the Lord promise that if we confess our sins, He is faithful and just to forgive us our sins and to cleanse us from all unrighteousness?

Woman: Yes.

Minister: And you have confessed your sins?

Woman: Yes.

Minister: Then according to the word of the Lord. you are forgiven, are you not?

Woman: That is just what I have been wanting to say for forty years.

Minister: Don't you believe the Bible?

Woman: Yes, certainly.

Minister: Well, does not the Bible say that if we confess our sins, He is faithful and just to forgive us our sins?

Woman: Yes.

Minister: Do you believe the Scripture?

Woman: Yes.

Minister: Have you confessed your sins?

Woman: Yes, over and over again.

Minister: Then, according to the word of the Lord, you are forgiven, aren't you?

Woman: That is just what I am afraid to say.

Minister: But does not the Lord say that if we confess our sins, He is faithful and just to forgive us our sins?

Woman: That is what He says.

Minister: What do *you* say? Dare you say that what He says is not so? Dare you say that you are *not* forgiven?

Woman: No, I dare not say that.

Minister: And you are afraid to say that you are forgiven? And you have lived in that state of mind for forty years?

Woman: Yes.

Minister: Are you sure you have confessed all your sins?

Woman: I have confessed all I know.

Minister: Would you confess another sin if it was shown you?

Woman: Most certainly.

Minister: But do you not know that your refusal to believe God is sin? The Word says, "He that believeth not God hath made him a liar" (I John 5:10). Now, stop calling God a liar, and believe that He forgives your sins. Let me help you over this Rubicon before which you have been standing in doubt for forty years. Say with me, "The Lord has forgiven my sins."

Woman: The Lord has—I am afraid.

Minister: Let us start again. The Lord has for——

Woman: I am afraid.

Minister: But you must believe God or perish. Let us back up and start in again. The Lord has forgiven——

Woman: I can't go any farther; let us pray.

And again we prayed, and prayed earnestly for deliverance from sin and unbelief, for the case was a desperate one. Again we rose from prayer. And again I repeated the words in concert with her. This time she followed me through, and then broke out in tears of joy over sins forgiven, a joy that she might have experienced forty years before, but for unbelief.

One has put it thus plainly and simply:

"You cannot atone for your past sins, you cannot change your heart, you cannot make yourself holy. But God promises to do all this for you through Christ. You *believe* that promise. You confess your sins, and give yourself to God. You *will* to serve Him. Just as surely as you do this, God will fulfil His word to you. If you believe the promise—believe that you are forgiven and cleansed—God supplies the fact; you are made whole, just as Christ gave the paralytic power to walk when the man believed that he was healed. It *is* so if you believe.

"Do not wait to *feel* that you are made whole, but say 'I believe it; it *is* so, not because I feel it, but because God has promised.'"

CHAPTER FOUR

YE ARE MY WITNESSES

After the devil had been cast out of the dweller among the tombs, this man wanted to get into the boat and accompany his great Deliverer, but the Master said to him, "Return to thine own house, and show how great things God hath done unto thee. And he went his way, and published throughout the whole city how great things Jesus had done unto him. And it came to pass, that, when Jesus was returned, the people gladly received him; for they were all waiting for him." Christ was leaving the neighborhood because the people asked Him to leave. However, He left behind Him a living witness of His power and compassion. He knew the people would hear this man, because they had known him before he was delivered, and could see how great things the Lord had done for him. He would prepare the way for the people to receive the Lord when He returned.

God has planned to save sinful men by the testimony of their fellow men. He has planned it this *way* because it is the best way. One reason for this is stated by another, thus:

15

"Many are perplexed with doubt, burdened with infirmities, weak in faith, and unable to grasp the unseen; but a friend whom they can see, coming to them in Christ's stead, can be a connecting link to fasten their trembling faith upon God."

The reason why the class or testimony meeting is often so poorly attended is that there are so few who have an experience worth telling. This is also the reason why so many complain of the embarrassment when called upon to witness for Christ.

"How many potatoes did you raise this year?" asks one farmer of another. "None to speak of," is the reply. He does not speak of his potato crop because he has none to speak of. And this is the reason why many do not speak of their experience; they have no experience to speak of.

Reader, if you do not have an experience to speak of, get one. If you already have an experience worth speaking of, then speak of it. "Ye are my witnesses, saith the Lord." Speak of it first in "thine own house" and then to your neighbors. God wants to use your testimony to save them. Your testimony will reach sinners when the Bible will not. "Likewise, ye wives, be in subjection to your own husbands; that, if any obey not the *word*, they also may *without the word* be won by the *conversation of the wives*; while they behold your chaste conversation coupled with fear" (I Peter 3:1, 2).

"Ye are the light of the world," says Christ. It is not the written Word that is the light of the world, because the world does not accept it. It is the Word made flesh that is the light of the world. Of Christ, who was the Word made flesh, it is written, "The life was the light of men." The written Word is a light to the Christian, but the Word made flesh is the light of the unbelieving world. It is the testimony of one in whom the Word is made flesh that the Spirit confirms with power for the conversion of sinners. One has stated this truth thus forcibly:

"After healing the woman, Jesus desired her to acknowledge the blessing she had received. The gifts which the gospel offers are not to be secured by stealth or enjoyed in secret. So the Lord calls upon us for confession of his goodness. 'Ye are my witnesses, saith the Lord, that I am God.'

"If we have been following Jesus step by step, we shall have something right to the point to tell concerning the way which He has led us. We can tell how we have tested His promises and found the promises true. We can bear witness to what we have known of the grace of Christ. This is the witness for which our Lord calls, for want of which the world is perishing.

"Our confession of His goodness is heaven's chosen agency for revealing Christ to the world. We are to acknowledge His grace as made known through the holy men of old, but that which will be most effectual is the testimony of our own experience. . . . These precious acknowledgments to the praise and glory of His grace, when supported by a Christlike life, have an irresistible power for the salvation of souls."

The reason, dear reader, why your testimony will be "more effectual" than the written testimony of the holy men of old, is because these holy men are *dead* and you are *alive*, and God's plan for reaching an unbelieving world is through the testimony of *living* witnesses. The holy men of God lived and witnessed in their day, and the record of their lives is a light to the believer, but the unbeliever must have the *life-light* of a living witness—the witness of the Word made flesh.

Reader, can you not see the value and importance of witnessing for Christ? It is your testimony which the Lord wishes to use to save your family and friends. Then tell your experience just as fast as God gives it to you.

Your experience is given you to tell. Tell it in your home and in your neighbors' homes. Tell it in the congregation. But be sure that it is backed up by a consistent life. Don't hide that comforting experience in your heart and rob the world of its comfort.

"I have not hid thy righteousness within my heart; I have declared thy faithfulness and thy salvation; I have not concealed thy lovingkindness and thy truth from the great congregation" (Ps. 40:10).

He who believes God, he whose heart holds a comforting experience, will declare it. If one refuses to confess with his mouth, he gives evidence that he does not believe with his heart. "Out of the abundance of the heart the mouth speaketh." "If thou shalt confess with thy mouth the Lord Jesus, and shalt believe in thine heart that God hath raised him from the dead, thou shalt be saved. For with the heart man believeth unto righteousness; and with the mouth confession is made unto salvation" (Rom. 10:9, 10).

It is blessed to have a good experience, but it is more blessed to give that experience to others. "It is more blessed to give than to receive." This I have found to be true in my experience. My greatest joy is found in giving to a sinning world the experiences which the Lord is giving me.

If there is anything that the devil fears, it is the testimony of a truly converted, Spirit-filled man. It is this that overcomes the enemy of truth. "And they overcame him by the blood of the Lamb, and by the word of their testimony" (Rev. 12:11).

Among those who stood and listened in the rear of a congregation of three thousand people was a minister who was not victorious in his life. At first, as he afterward related, he questioned the speaker's confident boasting in the Lord and His power to save, but as the witnessing continued, he believed, and said to himself: "Brother Ballenger is a man subject to like passions as I am. If God can save him, He can save me." At the close of the service he sought a secluded spot in the grove, and there gave himself to God, and sought and found the victory for which his soul hungered. This is but one of a multitude of cases where the writer's humble witness has been used by the Spirit to lead the listener to believe in and receive God's power to save to the uttermost. And this personal experience is related here to encourage the reader to bear faithful testimony to every experience gained through faith. As you read this little work and receive help from the Lord, tell it. Tell it in your home; tell it in your neighbor's home; tell it at prayer meeting; and if you have time, write it to the publishers. The chief joy of the Christian worker, who has turned his back on the joys of the world, is to hear of someone whom his words have helped to a better life. "Joy shall be in heaven over one sinner that repenteth, more than over ninety and nine just persons, which need no repentance." This joy of heaven is shared by the earth-accredited ambassador of heaven.

"Return to thine own house, and show how great things God hath done unto thee. And he went his way, and published throughout the whole city how great things Jesus had done unto him. And it came to pass, that, when Jesus was returned, the people gladly received him; for they were all waiting for him."

CHAPTER FIVE

PERSONAL EXPERIENCE IN RECEIVING
REPENTANCE AND FORGIVENESS OF SINS

At this point the writer asks of the reader the blessed privilege, and it is a *blessed privilege*, of bearing personal witness to the scriptural truth taught in the preceding pages.

I was a backslidden young minister. Through a failure to walk in the light, I had lost the liberty that there is in Christ. I had forgotten that I was purged from my old sins. I was a sinner, in need of salvation as much as any sinner that ever lived. But still I tried to preach.

Some poor sinning soul may think that this experience will not help him, because it begins with the experience of a minister, when he is only a common sinner. I was speaking in a mission at one time, and made the remark that it was far more difficult for God to save a backslidden preacher than to save a drunkard or a harlot.

"I don't want so much talk, I want proof," cried out a man on the front seat, who was slightly intoxicated. "Here it is," I replied. "Here is what the Saviour said to the preachers of Jerusalem: 'Verily I say unto you, That the publicans and the harlots go into the kingdom of God before you. For John came unto you in the way of righteousness, and ye believed him not; but the publicans and the harlots believed him; and ye, when ye had seen it, repented not afterward, that ye might believe him' (Matt. 21:31, 32)."

Yes, it is harder to reach a backslidden preacher than a harlot or a publican. Because when a man has donned a preacher's coat and cravat, and is engaged in the work of calling men to repentance, it is difficult for him to humble his heart in repentance. But there is only one path out of sin for preachers and publicans, and that is the path of repentance.

Not knowing my spiritual condition, some of my brethren in the ministry requested me to go to the help of a most needy congregation in a southern state and aid in conducting a series of revival services. I protested against going, giving every plausible reason, save the real one, which was my spiritual condition. After much urging, I consented.

As the train bore me on to my destination, the startling position in which I was placed was revealed to me. I was going to preach repentance to others while I myself was an unrepentant sinner. In my distress of mind I found temporary relief in the promise I made that I would never preach another discourse until I knew my sins were pardoned.

Early in the morning after my arrival, I excused myself from partaking of breakfast, and with Bible in hand sought a retired spot in an adjacent grove. And there I knelt and confessed my sins to God, and read His promises. The morning wore away and the hour for service—eleven o'clock—was drawing near. Over and over again I confessed my sins and asked for pardon in the name of Jesus, but saw no sign that I was heard.

I had come in contact with some who had laid great stress on physical demonstration in conversion, and I, too, looked for some such sign. I had heard of some who had seen a light when they were converted, and I looked up to the sun to see if there were not some peculiar appearance there that I could regard as a sign that I was heard and forgiven, but there was none. Some had said that they had heard a voice saying, "Thy sins are forgiven." I listened for such a voice, but heard none. I had also heard some say that they had felt a great internal change when they were converted, so I waited for this sign, but waited in vain.

It was nearing the hour of service, and I had declared that I would never preach again until I was forgiven. What should I do? Again I prayed and again I confessed my sins, but saw no sign of forgiveness. Then I turned and read this Scripture. "If we confess our sins, he is faithful and just to forgive us our sins, and to cleanse us from all unrighteousness" (I John 1:9). In my despair I said, "I have a mind to just believe that promise—just believe I am forgiven—for I have confessed my sins, and the Lord promises that if I will do this, He is faithful to forgive."

Then the devil grew frightened and suggested doubts and fears to my mind in this form: "Look out; if you say you are forgiven when you are not, it will be a lie, and you have sins enough without adding the sin of lying." "But what is a poor man to do?" I thought. "What more can I do? I have confessed my sins." "But suppose you have forgotten one," suggested the tempter. "If you say you are forgiven when you have omitted to confess a single sin, it will not be so, and you will add the sin of presumption to all the rest of your sins." "That is so," I said. "Suppose I have forgotten one sin, and have not confessed it, and then claim forgiveness, it will be false."

I was about to despair when the Lord by His Spirit came to my rescue with this Scripture: "Him hath God exalted with his right hand to be a Prince and a Saviour, for to *give repentance* to Israel, and forgiveness of sins" (Acts 5:31). And then I saw that the Lord had given me my repentance and it was my place to take the repentance and repent; that it was the Lord's work to give repentance, and when I had repented of all the sin revealed to me, that I was to have confidence that God had attended to His work well, and not charge Him with neglect or failure. It was the Lord's business to give me repentance, and it was my business to take repentance and repent. And it was the Lord's business to give me forgiveness of sins, and it was my business to take forgiveness of sins and be forgiven. I was willing to repent of any other sin that the Lord would reveal, and the Lord knew it. I was, therefore, to believe that He had been faithful and given me pardon for my sins. At this point I said, "Praise the Lord! He has forgiven my sins."

The tempter suggested this doubt, "Well, how do you *feel?* Do you feel any different?" "It is not a question of *feeling*, but a question of fact," I replied. "The Lord says if I confess my sins, He is faithful and just to forgive my sins, and I believe that He tells the truth; and what is more, I am going up to the congregation and tell them what He has done." Again the enemy was frightened. "Look out now," he suggested, "don't be a fanatic. Don't act foolish. If the Lord has forgiven you, the people will find it out without your telling them. And besides, what a disgrace on the ministry and the church for the people to learn that you had come to preach to them, and were yourself a sinner." "Get thee behind me, Satan," was my reply. "It is so, and I am going to give the Lord the glory by telling it to the people."

This I did, and then I had all the feelings that I could desire, and so did the congregation, which rejoiced with me that I was forgiven. But my *feelings*, my peace and joy, came as the *fruit* of *faith*, not my faith as a *fruit* of my *feelings*.

"Now the God of hope fill you with all *joy and peace in believing*" (Rom. 15:13). Joy and peace belong to those who believe, not to unbelievers. If the Lord should give peace and joy before we believed, we would be joyful and peaceful unbelievers; but joy and peace belong to believers, not to unbelievers.

This public confession was the beginning of a blessed revival. And I am persuaded that there are other blessed revivals which only wait for the repentance of the pastor. If the ministers are to lead the people, they must lead them in repentance and confession as truly as in other things. "Humble yourselves therefore under the mighty hand of God, that he may exalt you in due time."

I wish to emphasize the need of public testimony to what the Lord has done. "I have not hid thy righteousness within my heart; I have declared thy faithfulness and thy salvation; I have not concealed thy lovingkindness and thy truth from the great congregation" (Ps. 40:10).

CHAPTER SIX

THE SPIRIT CALLS FOR CONFESSION

"Confess your faults one to another." Why are we called upon to confess our faults one to another? It is so mortifying. Mortifying to what? Mortifying to the carnal heart. Well, don't you want the carnal heart mortified? It is only by mortifying the old life that the new life can appear. If there is a protest in your heart against confessing to your brother wherein you have wronged him, or to the church wherein you have reason to believe that your faults have affected the church or the public, you may depend upon it that that protest comes from a carnal heart which is fighting for life. Crucify it. Crucify it quickly. It is your only hope. It makes no difference who you are, whether officer or layman, prominent or obscure, crucify that carnal heart.

I was engaged in revival work in a certain city, and scores of people were seeking the forgiveness of sins and the blessings of a victorious Spirit-filled life. To my great surprise I was convicted by the Spirit of the sin of self-esteem. I was loath to believe it, but having learned not to argue with the Holy Spirit, I quickly surrendered and confessed the sin to God. Then I was impressed that I ought to confess it to the congregation, but immediately the objection was raised in my mind that such a course would hurt my influence with the people. But to this I replied that self-esteem cannot exist in the heart without manifesting itself in the life. Some discerning souls have seen it, and the only way to escape being a stumbling block in their paths is to confess it, and then they will see that the Spirit has succeeded in convincing me of it.

The next evening, after a short talk on the grace of humility and the sin of self-esteem, I confessed my fault to the congregation, and the Spirit so witnessed to the confession that nearly a hundred people were convicted of the same fault and made confession, supplicating with me for deliverance.

There had been in that congregation from night to night fathers and mothers in Israel with deep experiences, who were doubtless pained at the manifestation of the subtle pride in the young man, who, when that confession was made, praised the Lord that at last the Spirit had succeeded in convincing him of the sin, and had given strength to confess it and put it away. Confessing our faults one to another will not hurt our influence. "He that humbleth himself shall be exalted." "Humble yourselves therefore under the mighty hand of God, that he may exalt you in due time."

A young minister came to the writer with this sad complaint: "Whenever the Lord blesses me in my ministry, I become exalted over it, and He has to withdraw His power. What shall I do?" He was urged to con-

fess his pride to the Lord, and ask Him to crucify it;
then claim the crucifixion by faith in the promise of
God; then go before the congregation and confess his
pride there, and tell of the victory gained by faith. He
did so, and obtained the victory. Why, someone will
ask, must he confess it before the congregation? Because no one was ever proud without the people finding
it out. And when the people know that a man is proud,
that man will never gain the confidence of the people
until they know that he has discovered his pride and put
it away, and this they will know when he confesses it.
If he is too proud to confess his pride, then he has not
yet gained the victory over his pride.

That which is true of self-esteem is true also of all
other faults which are of a public character. There are
some things of such a character that they should never
be confessed in public; but there are others which are
more or less of a public nature that ought to be thus
confessed. Confessions should be frank. No attempt
should be made to excuse or palliate the wrong.

There was associated with me in a series of meetings in the west, a very earnest, conscientious, and
capable young minister. One night the Spirit convicted
many in the congregation of wrong-doing, and there
followed a confessing of faults one to another that
brought victory to many hearts. This young minister
arose and began a confession that evidently did not
meet the mind of the Spirit. Presently he stopped a
moment, and when he resumed his testimony he said:
"Brethren, I am convinced that I am trying to let myself down easy. I will stop and fall on the Rock and be

broken," which he immediately did, and the Lord witnessed by His Spirit to his whole-hearted confession.

It was at a meeting in the south. A middle-aged man, with gray hair and beard, arose in the meeting, and with great earnestness said: "I am a liar. I can't tell the truth. If I ever told you anything, you had better investigate it before you believe it."

There were many in the audience who could have said "amen" in confirmation of his statement, but they did not do it. Reader, have you not noticed that when a man or woman is making an honest confession of wrong-doing, even their worst enemies refrain from reproaching them?

"But I believe that I shall be able to tell the truth in the future, for I am receiving the Spirit of truth," continued the man. And there were many "amens" from tender hearts. Everybody seemed to forget that he had been a man given to exaggerating nearly everything he reported. It mattered not how he had been guilty of lying in the past; all had to admit that when he said he was a liar, he began to tell the truth. He began to be a truthful man when he confessed himself a liar, and he began to have a reputation for truth-telling in the community at the same time. By his confession he removed the reproach from himself and his church, and took his stand with the Lord, whose Spirit had convinced him of sin.

Reader, if you are a candidate for the baptism with the Holy Ghost, you must confess all your sins to God and your faults to your neighbor. All faults are sins;

but there are sins which lie between the individual and his God, and must be confessed to Him alone. Then there are sins which involve our fellows which must be confessed to them.

Commence today. Commence with your own family. If you are a father or mother, you may need to commence with one another or with the children. I covet, second to the confidence of the Lord, the confidence of my wife. If I cannot go before the people believing that she believes I am a Christian, I cannot go at all.

My father was called to minister in word and doctrine, but, like Jonah, he sought for a time to close his ears to the call and continue on the farm. Not following his convictions, he found it hard to maintain a victorious life, and consequently he said and did things at times which I could not harmonize with my conceptions of Christian living. And sometimes I was tempted to doubt his being a Christian, but when he came to me and said, "Son, I did wrong in that matter and I want you to forgive me," my confidence was restored, and I went away saying to myself, "There is no use in denying it; my father is a Christian." No parent ever lost the respect of the child by the frank acknowledgment of wrong-doing which involved the child. "He that covereth his sins shall not prosper: but whoso confesseth and forsaketh them shall have mercy."

CHAPTER SEVEN

THE SPIRIT CALLS FOR RESTITUTION

A pane of glass one-sixteenth of an inch in thickness, if placed between the transmitter and receiver, will baffle an electric current of sufficient strength to operate an entire streetcar system. "Behold, the Lord's hand is not shortened, that it cannot save; neither his ear heavy, that it cannot hear. *But your iniquities have separated between you and your God,* and your sins have hid his face from you, that he will not hear" (Isa. 59:1, 2). The "all-power-in-heaven-and earth" cannot penetrate past a single cherished sin.

"*Put away* the evil of your doings from before mine eyes; cease to do evil; learn to do well; seek judgment, relieve the oppressed, judge the fatherless, plead for the widow. Come, now, and let us reason together, saith the Lord; though your sins be as scarlet, they shall be as white as snow; though they be red like crimson, they shall be as wool" (Isa. 1:16–18).

A young man had come a long distance to attend the revival services. "I am glad to be here," he remarked; "I have heard of the good work done elsewhere, and it

33

is just what the people need; I hope you will give the message straight." His face beamed with satisfaction; he was interested in seeing the people benefited.

"I think I had better return home," he remarked to me the next day. His face bore a look of despair. "You came intending to remain throughout the meetings," I said. "It seems too bad to come so far and then return so soon. I think you had better stay." After a little hesitation he said, "I cannot stay. I cannot endure the presence of the Lord." "What is the trouble, my brother? Is there any wrong you are cherishing?" After a moment's thought he unburdened his heart thus:

"Five years ago, my neighbor deliberately turned his hogs into my cornfield. It angered me and, taking down my shotgun, I hurried out and shot one of them and tried to shoot more. When that hog died, I died. I have had no spirituality since; and this is no place for a man like me."

"Yes, it is," I replied, "if you will pay for the hog and make confession to the owner."

The value of the hog, with interest, was counted out, and then he said, "Ask the Lord to help me write a letter of confession, and I will send the money tonight." The letter was written, the money enclosed and mailed. Sin, the nonconductor, was removed, and the electric current of the Comforter thrilled his heart with a peace and joy that shone out in his face and was voiced in his public testimony.

The Spirit of God will not compromise with sin. He came to convince of sin, not condone it. "Thou shalt call his name Jesus; for he shall save his people from their sins" (Matt. 1:21).

Scores remained for the after-meeting, and as a result of personal work involving hard-fought, hand-to-hand battles with doubt and discouragement, nearly all found peace and joy in believing.

One remained still in unbelief. Our prayers seemed to avail nothing. We were still kneeling and silently waiting. Presently he whispered, "I would like to see you alone." A private interview revealed the fact that some years before he had been urged to prepare for active Christian work, and had received through the mail a check which, while its source was not indicated, he had reasons to know was sent for the purpose of helping him prepare for the ministry. This he had used for other purposes.

I exhorted him to restore the money. He replied that it was an impossibility at present.

"Is it in your heart to do it?" I asked. He answered, "Yes, just as soon as I can raise it." Will you show your faith by your works, and draw up a note and send it to the party with a confession of your wrong?" I continued. "Yes," was the reply. There was a moment of silence, and then, with a cry of joy, he threw his arms around me and we rejoiced together. That sin had acted as a nonconductor to the incoming of the Spirit with His message of pardon and peace. All our prayers were unavailing to bring the pardon until the sin was put away. Not until he had decided to restore that which he had misappropriated could he exercise faith for forgiveness. The work of restitution lies between many a soul and the comfort of the Holy Ghost.

"What shall I do?" said an earnest inquirer. "When a young man, I robbed my employer in small sums to the amount of about a hundred dollars. I have the money to restore, but I cannot find the merchant. I am afraid he is dead." I replied, "If the wronged one is dead, restore the money to his heirs. If there are no heirs, or they cannot be found, give it to the Lord. This is the teaching of the Word." This he did, and peace came.

There is another sin that is especially declared to be in the way of the pouring out of the overflowing blessing. "Will a man rob God? Yet ye have robbed me. But ye say, Wherein have we robbed thee? In tithes and offerings. Bring ye all the tithes into the storehouse, that there may be meat in mine house, and prove me now herewith, saith the Lord of hosts, if I will not open you the windows of heaven, and pour you out a blessing, that there shall not be room enough to receive it" (Mal. 3:8, 10).

Covetousness is the sin above all others that is keeping the power of God from many today. There is a growing desire to receive all that the church received in the early days of the pouring out of the Spirit. He who would approach the *receiving* of those days must approach the *giving* of those days.

Faith bars the door to sin, and sin bars the door to faith. "If our heart condemn us not, then have we confidence toward God. And whatsoever we ask, we receive of him, because we keep his commandments, and do those things that are pleasing in his sight" (I John 3:21, 22).

Many wonder why they cannot exercise faith, when the simple reason is the presence of the nonconductor, sin, which in the plan of God cannot be passed by until it is put away. Faith will come like the energizing electric current when there shall be a hearing of the Word, free from the clogging presence of cherished sin.

CHAPTER EIGHT

RIGHTEOUSNESS, THEN POWER

"Christ hath redeemed us from the curse of the law, being made a curse for us; for it is written, Cursed is every one that hangeth on a tree; that the *blessing of Abraham* might come on the Gentiles through Jesus Christ; that we might receive the *promise of the Spirit* through faith" (Gal. 3:13, 14).

"The promise of the Spirit" is the promise of the baptism with the Holy Spirit in its Pentecostal power. Just before His ascension Christ commanded His disciples "that they should not depart from Jerusalem, but wait for the *promise* of the Father, which, saith he, ye have heard of me. For truly John baptized with water; but ye shall be baptized with the Holy Ghost not many days hence. . . . Ye shall receive power, after that the Holy Ghost is come upon you." This promised baptism of power cannot be received by anyone who has not received the blessing of Abraham. For "the blessing of Abraham" is received "that we might receive the promise of the Spirit."

39

That the expression "the promise of the Spirit" is used by inspiration to mean the promise of God to give the Spirit, is very plain from Acts 2:33: "Therefore being by the right hand of God exalted, and having received of the Father the promise of the Holy Ghost, he hath shed forth this, which ye now see and hear." The expression "the promise of the Spirit," as used by Paul in Galatians 3:14, is identical with Peter's expression in Acts 2:33, "the promise of the Holy Ghost," which latter expression unmistakably points to the promise of God to give the Spirit.

Though receiving of the inheritance by faith is the theme of the chapter, it is perfectly consistent to understand the expression "the promise of the Spirit" as conveying the promise of God to give the Spirit, since the gift of the Spirit is an earnest, or first payment, on the inheritance. "After that ye believed, ye were sealed with that Holy Spirit of promise, which is the earnest of our inheritance until the redemption of the purchased possession" (Eph. 1:13, 14).

Reader, have you received the "blessing of Abraham"? It is useless to pray for the baptism with the Holy Spirit until you have. Do you know what the blessing of Abraham is? You may know, and know as quickly as Abraham knew, if you will do as Abraham did. Let us now go in search of the blessing of Abraham. The blessing of Abraham is the blessing of *righteousness* which God gave Abraham because he believed God when He spoke to him. Let us see that this is so. It is written (Gal. 3:6), "Abraham *believed* God, and it was accounted to him for righteousness." And again (verse 9), "So then they which be of faith [they that

believe God] are blessed with faithful Abraham."
Blessed with what? Blessed with what Abraham was
blessed with—blessed with righteousness. The blessing
of Abraham, therefore, is the blessing of righteousness
which the Lord gave to Abraham when He told Abraham He would do something for him that seemed impossible, and Abraham believed God *could* and *would*
do it (Gen. 15:6).

Now that you know what the blessing of Abraham
is for Abraham, God wants *you* to share in that blessing, to "be blessed with faithful Abraham," in order
that you may receive the promise of the Spirit.

Paul, in Romans 4:1–11, again shows that the blessing of Abraham is the righteousness with which God
blessed Abraham when he believed what God said.
Then the apostle makes a personal application of this
truth thus: "He staggered not at the promise of God
through unbelief; but was strong in faith, giving glory
to God; and being fully persuaded that what he had
promised, he was able also to perform. And therefore it
was imputed to him for righteousness. Now it was not
written for his sake alone, that it was imputed to him;
but for *us also*, to whom it shall be imputed, *if we believe* on him that raised up Jesus our Lord from the
dead; who was delivered for our offenses, and was
raised again for our justification" (Rom. 4:20–25).

"*If we believe.*" "They which be of *faith* [they that
believe] are blessed with faithful Abraham." Believe
what? Believe that God justifies (makes righteous)
the ungodly or unrighteous.

42

"But to him that worketh not, but believeth on him that justifieth the ungodly, *his faith* is counted for righteousness" (Rom. 4:5). Are you unrighteous, or ungodly? God says He will justify you, make you righteous, if you will ask Him to do it and believe that He does it.

"What things soever ye desire, when ye pray, believe that ye receive them, and ye shall have them" (Mark 11:24). Ask for the blessing of Abraham; ask God to forgive all the sins you ever committed from the day you knew the difference between right and wrong until this moment. Ask Him to give you the righteousness He has promised to give to the unrighteous. Then believe that you *have received that* righteousness. "For every one that asketh receiveth" (Luke 11:10).

"But," says someone, "if the blessing of Abraham is righteousness by faith, then I have always believed in that, for I have always believed in righteousness by faith." Good, if it is true. But if you have received righteousness by faith, you have stopped sinning. Righteousness by faith not only justifies you from your past sins, but saves you from falling into those same sins again. It is both a cure and preventive.

I am passing by my neighbor's house. He is in the cowyard milking. The cow kicks the milk over. The neighbor kicks the cow; then he seizes the stool and chases the cow around the yard. As he has the advantage in the inside track, he gets near enough to the cow to hurl the stool at her with telling effect. As my neighbor in his chase comes near the fence on which I am leaning, I speak thus: "Neighbor, have you accepted the message of righteousness by faith?"

He replies: "I have always believed in righteousness by faith; never believed anything else. And I think it is a disgrace to even suggest that we need a special message on this subject. What will our neighbors of the other churches think of us if they hear it? But what made you ask *me* if *I* believed in righteousness by faith?"

"Because when a man believes in righteousness by faith, he will not get angry and club his cow."

Reader, have you accepted righteousness by faith?—not the theory that men are made righteous by faith, but has it become a fact in your life? "Faith without works is dead." Do you still get out of patience in your home, at your work, with your brethren, with your neighbors, with your stock? Do you yield to the lusts of the flesh, to the lusts of the eye? Do you love the world, its goods, or its pleasures? Do you love the pre-eminence? The precious truth that men are made righteous and kept righteous by faith is given you to give you the victory over all your besetting sins. Then you will have received the blessing of Abraham, and can pray for the promise of the Spirit to make you a powerful witness for the truth. "Ask, and ye shall receive."

The following testimonies confirming the above truth have been received by letter:

"I wish to say the Lord gave me a precious wife; but since you left, I have a new one. A marked change has come to her. She is so patient. She has had a good test in moving. I hope she can see as great a change in me."

* * * * *

"When you were here, you spoke of having a new reputation in your father's family. Oh, how I wished I could say the same, as my father and I had trouble more than four years ago, and we were as far from a reconciliation as when the trouble first came up! You remember I spoke of writing some letters of confession, one of which was to my father. He responded, saying he freely forgave all, and that he would come to see me. True to his promise, he did come, although he had to travel four hundred miles. Thank the Lord, I now have a 'new reputation' with my father and all the family."

* * * * *

"Praise the Lord for victory, and for His keeping power! It is blessed to take God at His word; He is true. I can say to any who do not know the Lord, and to those who know Him but have not the victory over every besetting sin, 'Believe, have complete victory, and go on your way rejoicing.' "

CHAPTER NINE

"SIN NO MORE"

"Well," says someone, "if these are the qualifications necessary for receiving the Holy Ghost, I am afraid it will be a long time before I receive the witnessing power. I have been struggling for years to overcome my besetting sins, and if I get on no faster in the future, it will be years before I receive that power, if I ever do." But *you can get on faster*. You have been trying to gain the victory by the long-time process of *evolution*. Give up the theory of evolution, and accept the Bible doctrine of *creation*. "He spake, and it was done; He commanded, and it stood fast." Let Him speak to you, and have it done, and done so that it will stand fast. Once Christ spoke to a man and said, "Sin no more, lest a worse thing come unto thee." He did not say, "*Taper off* by the process of evolution through a long series of years, lest a worse thing come unto thee," but, "Sin no more." He speaks the same words to *you;* and He wants you to believe His word, and thereby be miraculously delivered from your sinning. Did you think it was necessary for you to taper off, or sin a little, in order to keep you from being exalted? Did you think you would have to fall into that same old sin occasionally in order that you might receive the grace of forgiveness? "Shall we continue in sin, that grace may abound? God forbid. How shall we that are dead to sin, live any longer therein?" (Rom. 6:1, 2). "Reckon ye also yourselves to be dead indeed unto sin, but alive unto God through Jesus Christ our Lord. Let not sin therefore reign in your mortal body, that ye should obey it in the lusts thereof. Neither yield ye your members as instruments of unrighteousness unto sin; but yield yourselves unto God, as those that are alive from the dead, and your members as instruments of righteousness unto God. For sin shall not have dominion over you" (Rom. 6:11–14).

Reader, stop right here and in faith ask God to break the dominion of sin over you. You can get the victory over every sin of which the Spirit has convinced you, in just the time it takes you to believe that God tells the truth when He says that sin shall not have dominion over you. "What things soever ye desire, when ye pray, believe that ye receive them, and ye shall have them" (Mark 11:24).

Hasten and get the victory. Hasten to get something to tell, and then you can ask God for power to tell it—for the baptism with the Holy Ghost.

Reader, if a drunkard should come to your church and apply for membership, stating the following conditions on which he would become a member, would you receive him? Listen, now, while he speaks, and decide:

"I hereby make application for membership in this church. But these are the conditions, and the only conditions, on which I will become a member. I am what is called a drunkard. For forty years I have been a slave to drink. And it isn't to be expected that I should quit all at once. I am willing to try to taper off; but of course I want plenty of time.

"When I get drunk, I generally whip my wife and break the furniture. Now I want this matter thoroughly understood, so that after I am a member and I get drunk and whip my wife, there must be no attention paid to it. I want it understood that I expect to get drunk and whip my wife for some time yet.

"But I will tell you what I will agree to do. Now I get drunk every day, but after I join the church I will agree to be sober half a day the next week, and be drunk only six days and a half. Then, after a time, I will keep sober one whole day, and be drunk only six days. After a time I will be sober two whole days, and get drunk only five. Later, I will be sober three days and drunk four; and then, after a while—but I want plenty of time—I will be sober four days and drunk only three days. Think of it, sober more than half of the time! After a long time I will get the advantage of this drink habit so that I will get drunk and whip my wife only on Saturday nights. And after a few years I will make such progress that I will get drunk only on Christmas, and New Year's, and Washington's Birthday, and Labor Day, and the Fourth of July, and Thanksgiving Day. Now, I have been forty years in forming this habit, and it will, of course, take some years to get rid of it.

"I make these statements so that after I join the church and get drunk and beat my wife, as I expect to do, no member of the church will have any reason to make a fuss about it. Now that it is distinctly understood that I expect to continue to get drunk and whip my wife for a time after I join the church, I present my application for membership, and ask for an immediate answer."

Now, reader, what will you do with this application? Will you vote to receive this man into your church?

So you unhesitatingly reject his application? Why do you refuse him membership? Because you don't receive drunkards and wife-beaters into the church? But what is the poor man to do?

"Stop drinking," do you say? Stop all of a sudden? Do you mean to say that you will vote to keep that man out of the church until he stops drinking and beating his wife? But he has been forty years contracting that habit. So you still insist on his stopping that terrible habit *instantly*? Do you mean to say that there is power enough in the gospel of Jesus Christ, which you profess, to give this poor man instant and permanent victory over his great enslaving sin so he need not get drunk and whip his wife any more forever? Your answer then, is, "Yes, emphatically, yes."

You have answered well. Your decision to exclude the drunken wife-beater until he is regenerated, and refuse to permit him to join the church and taper off, is a wise and scriptural decision. But now what are you going to do about your own case? What are you going to do with that besetting sin of yours? How long are you going to be in tapering off in your impatience, your evil thinking and speaking, your cruel criticizing, your fault-finding, your intemperance in eating, your pride of dress, your self-esteem, your love of the world, your love of worldly pleasure?

Can't you see that when you demand that the drunkard stop his drinking instantly, and declare that there is power in the gospel to thus deliver him, you condemn yourself, and are left yourself without excuse in continuing in your besetting sin another hour? And it was to bring you face to face with this solemn fact that this illustration was introduced. God *can* and God *does* deliver the drunkard and wife-beater instantly and permanently, and this is an evidence that you can be delivered instantly and permanently from your besetting sin.

When you shall come to look upon it in its true sinfulness, and become as desirous of deliverance as the drunkard, and seek God as earnestly, praying in faith, you too can have as immediate and permanent a deliverance. "Ask, and ye shall receive." "Sin shall not have dominion over you." "Go, and sin no more."

More confirming testimony from correspondence:

"I take pleasure in dropping you a few lines to tell you of my experience since you left. I had a hard fight with the devil during the entire meeting. I did not have that freedom I desired. I could not say, with the apostle Paul, 'There is therefore now no condemnation to them which are in Christ Jesus, who walk not after the flesh, but after the Spirit.' 'But thanks be to God, which giveth us the victory through our Lord Jesus Christ.' I praise the Lord that I have the victory over my besetting sin that has enslaved me for years; and now I can truly say that 'there is therefore *now* no condemnation to them which are in Christ Jesus.' I enjoy such freedom as I never before had in all my Christian experience.

" 'Blessed are they which do hunger and thirst after righteousness; for they shall be filled.' I can say that I have experienced that hungering and thirsting. Oh, praise the Lord for victory! This last week has been the most pleasant week of all my life, for I am gaining victories daily. I am not satisfied with anything short of having the fulness of the blessed Spirit. I have given myself to Him to be used to His glory. I drop you these lines, thinking they may be of some help to some other poor soul who is in bondage. Oh, praise the Lord for victory!"

* * * * *

"The good work begun still goes forward in my daily life. Complete victory is still my experience. As expressed in Isaiah 61:10, I can truthfully say I am 'joyful in my God; for he hath clothed me with the garments of salvation, he hath covered me with the robe of righteousness.' I have daily found great light and comfort in reading the books of Isaiah, Acts, and Romans. Two months ago I would have thought it an impossibility for me ever to grasp so quickly these wonderful victories and to have such uninterrupted peace."

CHAPTER TEN

SPEEDY DELIVERANCE

One of those who responded to the call to repentance was a middle-aged man who, though a member of the church, was a great sinner. At the close of the service he came to me with this question, "Do you mean to say that I can gain the victory over a besetting sin so completely that I need never commit that sin again?" "That is just what I mean," I replied. "Then I have never been a Christian, and never can be," was the desparing reply. "Not too fast, my friend," I replied. "As for the past of your life, I cannot speak; but as for what God can do in the future, I know if you will make a complete consecration, He can and will save you from your besetting sins, and so completely that you need be the slave of them no more forever."

As the meetings continued, he responded to every call to repentance, as one sin after another was seen in the light of the Spirit-illumined Word. During the day he went from house to house, confessing his faults and making restitution where he had wronged his neighbors. Confessions were made in his home, husband to wife, and wife to husband.   *3597*

His progress in spiritual things was astonishing. Every evening when opportunity was offered, he would make a confession to the congregation of some wrong which concerned the public, and which the Spirit had brought to his mind during the day, and then tell of the victory he was gaining over the powers of darkness. Such deliverance must have astonished and aroused the enemy, who counted upon him as forever ruined. At last Satan made a desperate effort to regain his control.

In the midst of the evening discourse, the deceiver suddenly threw upon him the memory of his life of sin, and ridiculed the idea of such a sinner ever being saved. He was staggered, then he doubted. Then the door was open for the devil, and he quickly followed his advantage with the suggestion that the only thing left was self-destruction; and the man immediately arose and started to leave the church to take his life. But the enemy wished to use him to divert the minds of the congregation from the discourse, and so he was thrown down in the aisle in a way to suggest the demon-possessed young man described in Luke 9:42.

He was carried staggering and groaning into the vestibule, where his distractions, cries and struggles continued. With the combined strength of eight men he was overpowered and carried to his home, from which he later escaped into the open fields; here he was again captured, and by the same number of men returned to his home.

So completely was he subject to Satan that at his suggestion, he, to all appearance, ceased to breathe, and the report was accordingly circulated that he was dead. But he again revived.

At the close of the service two ministers went to the house and, taking him by the hand, rebuked his unbelief, which manifested itself in expressions of despair, and quoted the promises of God. They were rewarded by seeing the man delivered from the devil.

At a following meeting he came into the congregation and related his experience and praised the Lord for his deliverance, saying that no devil-possession recorded in the Scriptures was more real than his.

From that time his help in the meetings was most valuable. Besides his ringing testimony borne every evening, which was always confirmed by that of his faithful wife, his personal work in talking and praying with sinners during the day and at the after service was a substantial aid to the work of the meetings.

His confessions and restitutions continued, and extended to other neighborhoods. He went to Boston and there acknowledged wherein he had wronged several business firms with which he had dealt. Not having the money to make immediate restitution, he gave them a list of his personal property, and told them to help themselves and satisfy their claims.

"How did they treat your offer?" I asked.

"Some took more than was their due, while others took less," he replied.

To this day this brand plucked from the burning has continued a faithful witness to the power of God to save the chief of sinners.

The purpose in relating this experience is to show how quickly God can take a great sinner who is willing, and give him complete and permanent deliverance from the dominion of Satan. The time it takes the Lord to accomplish a complete salvation is measured by that man's promptness in responding to the convicting and converting power of God. "Behold, the Lord's hand is not shortened, that it cannot save; neither his ear heavy, that it cannot hear; but your iniquities have separated between you and your God, and your sins have hid his face from you, that he will not hear" (Isa. 59:1, 2). "Only acknowledge thine iniquity" (Jer. 3:13). "If we confess our sins, he is faithful and just to forgive us our sins, and to cleanse us from all unrighteousness" (I John 1:9). "If the wicked restore the pledge, give again that he had robbed, walk in the statutes of life, without committing iniquity; he shall surely live, he shall not die" (Ezek. 33:15).

At the close of a service conducted with the students of an eastern academy, the preceptress brought a young lady student to me with the request that I make an effort to help her. The conversation was substantially as follows:

Minister: If the Lord Jesus sat where I am sitting, what would you ask Him for?

Student: I would ask Him for peace.

Minister: If He should offer you peace, would you take it?

Student: I would.

Minister: Are you entirely surrendered to the Lord?

Student: So far as I know, I am.

Minister: Do you know the Bible?

Student: Yes, indeed.

Minister: Do you believe it is the word of the Lord to *you*?

Student: Yes, sir.

Minister: Read the twenty-seventh verse of the fourteenth chapter of John. Read it aloud; I want to hear it. Remember it is peace you want.

Student: "Peace I leave with you, my peace I give unto you; not as the world giveth, give I unto you. Let not your heart be troubled, neither let it be afraid."

Minister: Do you believe that Scripture?

Student: I do.

Minister: Then the Lord has given you peace, hasn't He?

Student: He has.

Minister: Then let us kneel and thank Him for it.

After the prayer of thanksgiving, the young woman departed with joy, and time has shown a stable, steadfast Christian.

The two extracts from letters which follow are from the two parties referred to in this chapter:

"The Lord is still working for us at ———, and new victories are being won every day. The Lord is leading me and giving me a burden for others. I am spending most of my time with those who have not yet obtained the victory, but who have become interested and want to know more of the truth. I am growing stronger in the Lord every day. Praise His name that He can take such a poor, weak sinner as I was, and so fill him with the Holy Ghost that the Lord can use him to help poor sin-sick souls to gain the victory over Satan! I am so glad that the Lord is no respecter of persons. The Lord has worked a miracle for me, and I praise Him for it. The anchor holds. Glory to God, it holds! It is grounded on the solid rock of His salvation. I praise the Lord for His keeping power."

* * * * *

"Praise the Lord, the anchor still holds! 'Oh, how sweet to trust in Jesus, just to take Him at His word!' There is power in His word, and I see new beauties in John 14:27. I also know what Romans 8:1 means. The Bible is a new book. I cannot refrain from singing praises to God continually. The peace of God passes all understanding. When Auntie asked me if I did not wish to have a little talk with you, I told her it would be of no use; but I see now how great a hold Satan had on me. So, who has a greater right to shout victory and praise to Jesus than I?"

A fashionable young woman appeared in the congregation at a revival meeting. She was conspicuous because of her millinery, which, while in good taste viewed from the standpoint of the world, was in contrast with the plainer attire of most of the congregation.

I noticed her listening closely, but thought she was only a respectful transient visitor. She came again. I said to myself, "If that young woman continues to attend the services, she will eventually leave that hat at home." And so it was. And then came a request for an interview and for prayer. "And what shall I pray for?" I asked. "Pray that the Lord will give me strength to surrender," was the response. "I will," I replied. "But will you not join with me in this prayer?" "I cannot pray," was the reply. "You certainly can ask God to help you surrender."

She did not promise to do it, but I knelt and prayed. After some time of silence she prayed one sentence— a request for strength to surrender all. And it was done. And then there was great joy in that surrendered heart.

"Why cannot I be healed?" was the next question. "My health is very poor." The answer was that she could if she had faith to be healed. She was given a number of Scriptures to study, with the instruction that, if faith came from hearing these Scriptures, she was to call for the elders, and they would proceed according to the instruction found in James.

Later she called for anointing and prayer. After a careful questioning to ascertain if she "had faith to be healed" so that we might pray "the prayer of faith," we prayed over her, anointing her with oil in the "name of the Lord." When the prayers were ended, and we had arisen, she remarked with a calm confidence, "I believe I am healed, but I feel no change." Presently she said, "Let us kneel and thank the Lord for my healing."

Such faith from one so newly converted was refreshing. She was asked to lead in the thanksgiving, which she did with a freedom and fervor which deeply impressed all present. When we again arose she quietly remarked, "Now I feel the healing power."

Her *healing* and *feeling* had *followed* her *faith*, and now she had healing and joy and peace in believing. Someone may say, "Now I know the formula; now I will pray for the Holy Spirit or for healing, and then get up and say, I am filled, or I am healed, and it will be so." No; *saying* that it is so will not make it so. If it is said in *faith*, it is so; but if it is said in *form*, it is not so. Faith is not *created by* one's *will-power*. *Faith comes by hearing the Word of God.* And unless *faith comes*, the formula, the prayer, the anointing and the laying on of hands, will avail nothing.

If anyone lacks faith, let him continue to *hear the Word*. And when faith comes, he will know it. He will not need anyone to tell him whether he has faith; and the minister who is acquainted with faith will recognize that faith.

"What is your trouble?" was asked of a man who had remained for the after-meeting. "I want to be a Christian, but I am afraid to start for fear I will fall," was the response.

"If the Lord should speak to you with an audible voice from heaven and tell you not to fear, that He would hold you up, would you start?" "Yes," was the answer.

"Do you believe that the Lord speaks to men through the Bible?" "I do." "Do you believe that He speaks to you?" "Yes." "Then read the tenth verse of the forty-first chapter of Isaiah and hear Him speak to you."

He read: "Fear thou not; for I am with thee: be not dismayed; for I am thy God. I will strengthen thee; yea, I will help thee; yea, I will uphold thee with the right hand of my righteousness."

"I will start," said the man when he had finished reading, and there appeared in his face a new-born confidence in God's willingness and ability to uphold him.

CHAPTER ELEVEN

PERSONAL EXPERIENCE
IN RECEIVING KEEPING POWER

The writer wishes to bear witness to the faithfulness of the Lord in fulfilling the promise of His Word, not only to forgive sin, but to keep one from falling back into the same old sins again.

He has learned by experience that while the gift of forgiveness of sins is a blessed gift, it is not the end but only the beginning of Christian experience. "Many shall be purified, and made white, and *tried*" (Dan. 12:10). After the taking away of sin, then comes the testing. After conversion, then character-building. Some seem surprised that they should meet with great trial after conversion; but this is not strange. "Think it not strange concerning the fiery trial which is to try you, as though some strange thing happened unto you."

After conversion when I met with sore temptation, I was surprised and repeatedly overcome. I had learned the Lord's willingness to forgive, and would hasten to confess my sin and receive forgiveness, and start again with strong determinations and bright hopes, only to fail again. This sinning and repenting continued until I grew so tired out and so humbled by it, and so hungry for victory, that I was willing to be taught by the humblest instrument whom the Lord would use.

In this condition of mind I was providentially led into a mission in one of our large cities. It was my plan to remain a spectator, to secure what good I could, and depart without disclosing my identity.

The leader of the meeting read a short Scripture, made a few practical comments, and then began *witnessing* to the faithfulness of God to fulfill His promises. "Three years ago tonight," said the speaker, "I came into this mission a slave to drink. I was bankrupt physically, morally, and financially. If salvation had cost only a cent, I could not have gotten it. I had heard that a man would find friends in the mission when all other friends had forsaken him. I listened to the testimonies of the other men who said they had been saved from drunkards' graves through faith in Jesus Christ, and I made up my mind to give myself to the Lord and ask Him to save me. I did, and He saved me. I have not drunk a drop of liquor, nor used tobacco, nor sworn an oath since that night. My wife and children, who had been scattered by my life of drunkenness and sin, have been gathered again, and we are now a united family. Morning and evening we have our family worship where we join in praising the Lord for His salvation."

The witnessing of this poor publican thrilled me through and through. Hasn't touched a drop of liquor, nor used tobacco, nor sworn an oath for three years!

"*There* is something *permanent*," I said to myself. "Why can I not be saved from my besetting sins in that same way? Why can I not be saved from my impatience with a salvation just as permanent as that?"

The witnessing of this man so thrilled me that I seemed full of amens, but I did not intend to allow my identity to be known, and so smothered them.

"I was raised in the Bowery," said another man, "and sold papers for a living, and slept in the alley and in the dry-goods boxes. When I grew older, I stole for a living, and then I gambled for a living, and drank and fought and committed all the other sins which go along with such a life until I was a wreck without hope. In my despair I came into this mission, just five years, three months, and twenty-one days ago tonight, where I sought the Lord for salvation, and He saved me. I have not stolen, nor gambled, nor fought, nor drunk since that night. Praise the Lord! And what He has done for me, He will do for any sinner here."

"There, that is what I want; something permanent," I thought to myself. "Why can I not be saved from my besetting sins in just that way? Five years, three months, and twenty-one days! Why is he so definite about the time? He must greatly appreciate every day that he is saved from his old sins. Why don't I count my salvation by the day? I wonder if these poor fellows really appreciate their salvation more than I do. But they have been saved from such terrible lives, they ought to be thankful. Then the reason why I am not more thankful for my salvation is because I don't think my salvation is very remarkable, and the reason why it is not very remarkable is because I was not in need of a very remarkable salvation, because I have not been a very remarkable sinner." "To whom little is forgiven, the same loveth little" (Luke 7:47).

Then I found myself arm in arm with that other Pharisee who was found praying with that other publican in the temple. The Pharisee said, "God, I thank thee that I am not as other men are, extortioners, unjust, adulterers, or even as this publican."

The publican said, "God be merciful to me a sinner." Jesus said, "I tell you, this man went down to his house justified rather than the other" (Luke 18:11, 13, 14).

The one went away glorifying God for his salvation, the other remained glorifying himself in his self-righteousness. When I saw the company I was in, I immediately broke with the Pharisee and moved closer to the publican. I wanted a great salvation. I wanted it at any cost.

"Five years, eleven months, and sixteen days ago tonight, I came into this mission a ragged, penniless, ruined man. I had decided to throw myself in the river, but I thought I would stop in here first. That night the Lord saved me from my drink and sin, and for over two years I was a sober man. But after I had secured a good position and began to wear good clothes, I began to think I was able to walk alone, and I let go of the hand that had saved me and kept me, and I fell back into the old life again. But I knew I was down, and I knew how I was saved before. The Lord saved me again, and has kept me ever since; and I don't let go of His hand any more."

I wanted to say, "Amen," but again I smothered it.

Presently a woman arose. She was dressed in white. Some friends had brought her a large bouquet of white lilies. They had come to rejoice with her, to celebrate with her the fifth anniversary of her salvation from a life of sin and shame.

"Five years ago tonight," the young woman began. "I was rescued from a life of sin and shame. The Lord saved me from the street when I was engaged in the work of destroying the sons and daughters of fond mothers. But the Lord found me and washed me clean in His own blood. I have since started a rescue home, and I am now giving my life to the work of rescuing my sisters from the life which the Lord has rescued me. Oh, what a change He has wrought in my heart! Yesterday, with some Christian friends, I spent a day of recreation in the park and, would you believe it? I had entrusted to me, during the day, twelve little sweet-faced girls. Oh, think of it; that such a woman as I have been should be so cleansed and changed that mothers would be willing to trust me with the care of their innocent little ones! Praise the Lord for His love and saving power!"

I could smother the amens no longer, and one escaped with a good church prayer meeting fervor.

The people looked around. I could hide my identity no longer, but arose and said:

66

"Brethren and sisters, I am a preacher; but I see a salvation manifested here that I have not experienced. But I purpose to have it if I must get drunk, get arrested, and sentenced to jail and have some missionary come and teach me through the bars. I must have it at any cost. The Lord is no respecter of persons. If He can save you from your besetting sins and keep you saved, He can save me from mine."

I went from this meeting to my home strongly impressed with God's power to save to the uttermost. I looked myself over in the light of the Word and decided that I was mean enough already; that I need not sin any more in order to be a great sinner and obtain a great salvation. I found my heart described in the Word as "desperately wicked," and that a salvation from such a desperately wicked heart would be a glorious salvation. Some of this wickedness had worked its way out, and I had seen it and was willing to take by faith the truthfulness of the Word for all that had not been seen.

Then I found myself, in my own estimation, beside the penitent publican, and I too asked to be saved like any other publican. I claimed salvation from my besetting sins by faith just as the other publicans and just as I had claimed the forgiveness of sins on a former occasion. I based my faith on the promise of the Word that, having yielded my members "as instruments of righteousness unto God," "sin shall not have dominion over you" (Rom. 6:13, 14). I claimed it without any other evidence except the promise of God. I claimed it by faith. "What things soever ye desire, when ye pray, believe that ye receive them, and ye shall have them" (Mark 11:24).

Then I went to the mission meeting and related my experience and told them that I found I did not need to become a drunkard to be bad enough to be in need of a great salvation; that I had found I was mean enough already. Seeing this, I had sought salvation from my besetting sins just like any other great sinner, and had found the Saviour who saves to the uttermost; and from this time on I did not propose that any converted drunkard or harlot should ever excel me in praising the Lord for salvation.

Thus, dear reader, did I learn through this humbling experience the secret of a great salvation. Only those who realize that they are great sinners will receive a great salvation. Sin as seen nailing the Son of God to the cross of Calvary becomes exceedingly sinful.

Remember, it was such a view of sin, a complete consecration of all to God and faith in the naked promise of God to save to the uttermost and keep the sinner from falling, that wrought this deliverance.

CHAPTER TWELVE

HUMILITY, THEN GLORY

"Whom he *justified*, them he also *glorified*" (Rom. 8:30). Why is it that the message of justification by faith, or the blessing of Abraham, must be received before the promise of the Spirit, or the baptism with the Holy Ghost, can be received (Gal. 3:14)? One reason is that the reception of the truth that we are made righteous and kept righteous by faith is a complete and everlasting destruction to the thing which, above every other thing, is keeping the baptism with the Spirit from the church. That thing is *pride*. Self-pride, family pride, church pride, state pride, national pride—it matters not in what form it appears; pride is a barrier to the promise of the reception of the Spirit. But the reception of the gospel message of righteousness by faith is instant and eternal death to all the pride of every human heart that fully receives it.

"If Abraham were justified by works, he hath whereof to *glory;* but not before God." If you could justify yourself by your good works, you would have whereof to glory; but you cannot, and when you really

69

come to believe this, all self-glorying, all pride will depart from the heart. "For all have sinned, and come short of the glory of God; being justified freely by his grace through the redemption that is in Christ Jesus; whom God hath set forth to be a propitiation through faith in his blood, to declare his righteousness for the remission of sins that are past, through the forbearance of God; to declare, I say, at this time his righteousness; that he might be just, and the justifier of him which believeth in Jesus. *Where is boasting then? It is excluded*" (Rom. 3:23–27).

All boasting is excluded from the heart which has come to realize that righteousness is alone by faith. But why is this so? What is the divine philosophy of it? Here it is: If righteousness is of faith, not of works, then it cannot be *earned;* it must be *begged.* Justification by faith, therefore, makes a beggar of every sinner; and as "all have sinned," it makes beggars of the whole human race, rich and poor, high and low, wise and unwise. And when men and women are brought to the place where they feel their need so keenly that they will humble themselves to beg, it is to be expected that their pride is crucified.

When we seek to be justified by faith, we must come to the Lord and acknowledge that we are unjust, that we are sinners, that we need to have our sins forgiven. This is humbling to the natural heart. By this coming we acknowledge that we cannot make ourselves righteous; we cannot forgive our own sins. If we could, we would not have come. And this, too, is humbling. And when we come, we have to ask forgiveness as a beggar would have to ask for food at the door. "Knock and it shall be opened unto you"; "ask, and it shall be given you." And this, also, is humbling. And should we be asked what we have to pay for it, we must reply that we haven't anything to pay, but that the Lord Jesus told us that if we would come and ask help in His name, it would be given us *free*. And this is humbling, too.

All this is but a small part of the humbling. We must ask for a fresh supply every day; we cannot come and get a supply that will last forever so that we can go away and be independent of the Giver, and become proud and self-righteous over what has been given us. We are compelled to acknowledge that we cannot keep ourselves from falling into those same sins for which we have been forgiven. We have to ask the Lord for daily bread, for strength to keep us from falling, and tell Him again and again that we have nothing to pay, but the Saviour told us to come and ask for keeping power in His name and it would be given *free*. Yes, we have to come and ask to be fed *free* all the time, to become regular charity boarders. And if we ever get the idea that we are earning our living, that we are not any longer charity boarders, or, in other words, that we can keep ourselves from falling into our old sins, there must come a terrible fall which, like David's, will break our bones and bring forcibly to mind the fact of our dependence on Him who alone is able to keep us "from falling." Yes, the gospel truth that men are made righteous by faith humbles the glory of man in the dust. It teaches him that he cannot forgive his own past sins, but must come to the Lord and ask forgiveness, and must take it by faith. It teaches him also that he cannot keep himself from falling into those old sins again, but he must come and ask for keeping power and then believe that he receives it and be thankful for it.

Reader, has the gospel of righteousness by faith done this work of humbling for you? Is all your pride crucified? Is your own glory in the dust? Are you ready to be glorified with "power from on high"? Should you be baptized with the Holy Ghost for witnessing power, could you keep humble while the multitude looked on in wonder and amazement? Should the cripple be healed and begin leaping and shouting and the people flock around and look at you with awe and admiration, would you say from the *heart*, "Why look ye so earnestly on *us*, as though by our own power or holiness we had made this man to walk?"

Would you point them to the Lamb of God that taketh away the sin of the world? The gospel of righteousness as a free gift is sent to you to humble you and prepare you to be glorified.

There is much being written and spoken today concerning the Holy Spirit. Many prayers are offered at conventions and conferences for the baptism with the Holy Spirit. But God is merciful and does not grant the request, because to do so would be to bring ruin to the receiver. Should the Lord grant apostolic power to one who is proud, He would thereby feed that pride. A proud man with power is a foe to himself, his God, and his fellows. Satan is a startling example of the results of pride with power.

God is anxious to baptize men and women with the Holy Ghost and power. But they must first be humble. The apostles were men from the humble walks of life, but still they had to be humbled. Paul's converts were men who were led to turn from the "foolish things" of the world, but he exhorted them to humility thus: "For ye see your calling, brethren, how that not many wise men after the flesh, not many mighty, not many noble, are called; but God hath chosen the foolish things of the world to confound the wise; and God hath chosen the weak things of the world to confound the things which are mighty; and base things of the world, and things which are despised, hath God chosen, yea, and things which are not, to bring to nought things that are: *that no flesh should glory* in his presence. But of him are ye in Christ Jesus, who of God is made unto us wisdom, and righteousness, and sanctification, and redemption; that, according as it is written, he that glorieth, let him *glory in the Lord*" (I Cor. 1:26–31). "But God, who is rich in mercy, for his great love wherewith he loved us, even when we were dead in sins, hath quickened us together with Christ (by grace ye are saved); and hath raised us up together, and made us sit together in heavenly places in Christ Jesus; that in the ages to come he might show the exceeding riches of his grace in his kindness toward us through Christ Jesus. For by grace are ye saved through faith; and that not of yourselves; it is the gift of God; not of works, *lest any man should boast*" (Eph. 2:4–9). "For who maketh thee to differ from another? and what hast thou that thou didst not receive? now if thou didst receive it, why dost thou *glory*, as if thou hadst not received it?" (I Cor. 4:7).

While pride is the sin above every other sin that is keeping the baptism with the Holy Spirit away from men and women, yet it is easy for God to destroy it. Ask

Him to do it. Believe that He does it, and it is done. Accept righteousness by faith and you will be humbled. When humbled, you are ready to be exalted with power from on high (I Peter 5:6).

CHAPTER THIRTEEN

THE SPIRIT IN SANCTIFICATION

She had prayed earnestly to the Lord to show her the true condition of her heart. When He gave her a glimpse of its real condition, though a Christian worker, she immediately went into hopeless despair, and a stupor with alarming indifference took possession of her.

At this point, with other ministers I was requested by her friends to visit her. Our earnest inquiry called out the foregoing facts, but all efforts to get her to seek the Lord for deliverance failed for a time. A part of the conversation was in substance as follows:

Minister: So you asked the Lord to show you the sinfulness of your heart?

Woman: Yes.

Minister: And He heard your prayer and revealed your sinfulness?

Woman: Yes.

Minister: Why did you sink into this discouragement?

Woman: Because I despaired of ever being saved from my sinfulness.

Minister: But did you not ask Him to show you your sinfulness?

Woman: Yes.

Minister: Is not your despair the result of your doubting the power and love of God to save you from the sins you asked Him to show you?

Woman: I presume it is.

Minister: Have you not sinned in doubting God's love and power?

Woman: I presume I have.

Minister: Will you repent of that sin?

Woman: I can't.

Minister: Will you kneel here and ask the Lord to forgive you for doubting His love?

Woman: I cannot pray.

All these answers were made in a dazed, indifferent way.

After much urging, the woman knelt. But she seemed unable to pray. Though a Christian worker, she seemed powerless to pray the simplest prayer. She was asked to repeat this prayer, "O Lord, forgive me for doubting Thy love."

Before she had finished the sentence, the spell was broken, and she wept tears of repentance from eyes which before were dry and hopeless, while the minister finished the sentence with a prayer of thanksgiving.

A marvelous transformation followed, and hope and joy returned. We may indeed thank the Lord that He does not reveal to us all of our imperfections at once.

"Will you not come and speak with a young woman who, I fear, is losing her interest in the meetings?" was a request which came to me at the close of a service in the west.

In response to an inquiry, the young woman related how, the day before, she sought the Lord with others at the revival service, and had found forgiveness and peace. But while still kneeling, the Lord had revealed a sacrifice which He called upon her to make. But she was not willing to surrender her idol, and she charged God with a lack of love in calling upon her so quickly to make this surrender. "He ought to have waited until I was stronger," she boldly declared.

All attempts to renew her interest in her salvation were futile. She had refused to permit the Lord to lead her further. She had grieved the Spirit by her rebellion, and she was left without conviction.

How careful the Lord is in the work of wooing the sinner from his sins, and yet with all His love and wisdom many refuse to be led in the path of self-denial.

Bible sanctification is a progressive work. We cannot bear to see all of our wrong-doing at once; and no wrong-doing will ever be righted until the wrong-doer is able to see the wrong-doing as wrong, and deliberately decide against it and seek God for deliverance from it. God does not arbitrarily deliver us from sin. God does not deliver us from sin without our knowledge, consent, and cooperation. How could He? How could I be saved from wrong-doing while not knowing it to be wrong? If I do not know a thing to be wrong, I must regard it as right. How can God ever save me from a wrong-doing which I consider right-doing unless He can first show me that the thing is wrong? Perfect sanctification necessitates perfect knowledge of right and wrong. The acquiring of this knowledge requires time. It is gained by experience, by exercise, or training. All this is taught in the following Scripture:

"For when by reason of the time ye ought to be teachers, ye have need again that some one teach you the rudiments of the first principles of the oracles of God; and are become such as have need of milk, and not of solid food. For every one that partaketh of milk is without experience of the word of righteousness; for he is a babe. But solid food is for full-grown men, even those who by reason of use have their senses exercised to discern good and evil" (Heb. 5:12–14, R.V.).

A full-grown man, therefore, is a man of experience—one who, because of having used his spiritual faculties, has them exercised, or trained, to discern good and evil. All this proves that we must be able to discern evil before we shall be able or willing to put it away. And this perfect discernment is the fruit of experience, or spiritual exercise. It cannot all be acquired in a moment.

Our Lord spoke the gospel to the people "as they were able to hear it." And to His disciples He said, "I have yet many things to say unto you, but ye cannot bear them now" (John 16:12). Just as fast as any man is able to bear the truth, God will reveal it to him, and just as fast as he is able to receive the truth, just so fast is he being sanctified by it. It is the office of the Holy Spirit to guide men into all truth by revealing to them the word of truth. "Sanctify them through thy truth; thy word is truth" (John 17:17). "When he, the Spirit of truth, is come, he will guide you into all truth; for he shall not speak of himself; but whatsoever he shall hear, that shall he speak" (John 16:13).

But while sanctification is a progressive work, for the reason that man is not able to bear the sight of all his imperfections at once, yet the deliverance from an imperfection which the Lord has revealed is not a progressive but an instantaneous work. To illustrate: When the Lord convicts men that the use of tobacco is sinful, He does not want them to taper off. He does not intend that they shall continue for a moment to do, in the smallest particular, that which they know to be sin. "If I had not come and spoken unto them, they had not had sin; but now they have no excuse for their sin" (John 15:22, R.V.). "Jesus said unto them, If ye were blind, ye should have no sin; but now ye say, We see; therefore your sin remaineth" (John 9:41). "Therefore to him that knoweth to do good, and doeth it not, to him it is sin" (James 4:17).

There is therefore no excuse for anyone's continuing in a sin which he has been shown by the Spirit to be sin. God says that he is without excuse. And the reason that he is without excuse is that when God gives a knowledge of sin, He always furnishes with that knowledge the power to triumph over sin. "The law came in besides, that the trespass might abound; but where sin abounded, grace did abound more exceedingly; that, as sin reigned in death, even so might grace reign through righteousness unto eternal life through Jesus Christ our Lord. What shall we say then? Shall we continue in sin, that grace may abound? God forbid. We who died to sin, how shall we any longer live therein?" (Rom. 5:20, 21; 6:1, 2, R.V.).

Reader, are you walking in the light? Are you gaining victories at every step, and are you stepping fast? The Spirit exhorts us thus: "Wherefore let us cease to speak of the first principles of Christ, and press on unto perfection; not laying again a foundation of repentance from dead works" (Heb. 6:1, R.V.). God has planned that the Christian experience shall be one long series of glorious victories over the world, the flesh, and the devil, from Christian birth to Christian perfection. When, in our upward march, a hitherto undiscovered sin appears in the path of progress, there is no excuse for ever being overcome by that sin again, nor for being halted by it for a moment. The God who points out the sin, furnishes power, in response to faith, for instant and everlasting victory over that sin. "There is therefore now no condemnation to them which are in Christ Jesus, who walk not after the flesh, but after the Spirit. For the law of the Spirit of life in Christ Jesus hath made me free from the law of sin and death" (Rom. 8:1, 2).

CHAPTER FOURTEEN

THE HOLY SPIRIT AND THE
UNPARDONABLE SIN

Not only is there no excuse for continuing in sin after it is known to be sin, but it is a fearfully danger- ous thing to do. This habit of sinning and repenting, this "going forward" and "backsliding" involves the committing of the unpardonable sin.

The apostle, after telling the Hebrews that they needed to be taught again the first principles of Chris- tian experience when, considering the time they had confessed Christ, they ought to be teachers of others, urges them to press on unto perfection. The reason for this earnest exhortation is given in these solemn words which follow: "For it is impossible for those who were once enlightened, and have tasted of the heavenly gift, and were made partakers of the Holy Ghost, and have tasted the good word of God, and the powers of the world to come, if they fall away, to renew them again unto repentance; seeing they crucify to them- selves the Son of God afresh, and put him to an open shame. For the earth which drinketh in the rain that cometh oft upon it, and bringeth forth herbs meet for

them by whom it is dressed, receiveth blessing from
God; and is nigh unto cursing; whose end is to be
burned" (Heb. 6:4–8).

God does not arbitrarily reject any sinning soul.
When the oft-repeated showers of His grace produce no
permanent fruit, but in the place of fruit there appear
only thorns and thistles, there is nothing left but rejection and burning. Reader, have you been enlightened
about your besetting sins? Have you tasted the Word
of God, its cleansing and keeping power? Do you know
how to be victorious through faith in His promise?
Have you experienced this victory? Then it is a fearfully dangerous thing for you to backslide and bear
briers and thorns. If we bear thorns when we know
they are thorns, and when we know the power of God
to bear the fruits of the Spirit, what more can God
do than He has done to save us from the thorns? What
possible course is left to God but rejection and destruction? All He has to produce the fruits is showers; but
after all the showers only thorns! The whole matter is
summed up in this one sentence, "Press on or perish."
Backslidings must end. Sinning must cease. But still
there is hope—yes, hope for those who, by reason of
the time they have been professing Christians, ought to
be teachers, and are still in need of being taught the
first principles of Christian experience.

It was to this very class of backsliders that the Word
was speaking when it urged them to "press on unto perfection." To these very backsliders it expressed hope;
to these who were so very near to committing the unpardonable sin it says, "But, beloved, we are persuaded

better things of you, and things that accompany salvation, though we thus speak" (Heb. 6:9).

Beloved, let us press on unto perfection. We must press on or perish. But how shall I press on? If you are not pressing on, it is because you have come up to some test in your life, and failed to meet that test and overcome through faith in the promise of God to give you the victory. What is that test? What is that sin you have failed to put away by the power of God? Or, if it be more than one, what are those sins? Confess them to God. If they are sins that have wronged others, "confess your faults one to another." Do it now. If the wronged ones cannot be reached in person, write them a letter of confession. Do it quickly. The devil says, "Put it off"; the Spirit says, "Do it today." Having confessed your wrongs, ask to be forgiven. You have the promise of God that, this done, He will forgive. With the forgiveness, ask also for power to overcome your besetting sins. Ask and ye shall receive. "This is the victory that overcometh the world, even our faith." "What things soever ye desire, when ye pray, believe ye receive them, and ye shall have them." It is so if you believe it. Do not wait to feel that you are made whole. But say, "I believe it; not because I feel it, but because God has promised it." Having done this, now bear testimony that it is done. "If you believe the promise—believe that you are forgiven and cleansed—God supplies the fact; you are made whole."

CHAPTER FIFTEEN

SECRET OF REJOICING IN TRIBULATION

We are commanded to rejoice in tribulation. This does not mean that we must rejoice in tribulation in the sense of enjoying tribulation, for we are told in another place that "all chastening seemeth for the present to be not joyous, but grievous" (Heb. 12:11, R.V.). It is presented as something to be endured ("if ye endure chastening"), not something to be enjoyed. We are to rejoice while in tribulation, but not in tribulation itself. But why are we to rejoice while in tribulation? Because of what the tribulation is accomplishing for us. "Tribulation worketh patience; and patience, experience; and experience, hope" (Rom. 5:3, 4). No one has any real enduring hope of salvation either for himself or anyone else unless he has endured tribulation. and thereby obtained an experience.

Experience is the Christian's capital. It is "more precious than gold that perisheth." The fiercer the flame, the purer the gold; so the more testing the trial. the more precious the experience. Reader, how much of this gold have you in heaven's bank? Do you not

85

greatly rejoice over what you have? If what you have makes you so happy, ought you not to be happy over the prospect of getting more? If you really knew that you were right in the act of getting more of this gold of experience, ought you not to be glad? Were you not glad the last time you were so sorely tempted to be impatient, selfish, or proud, or envious, or unclean in thought or act, that you had a glorious opportunity to stand the trial and thus add another victory to your stock of experience? Then, do not ever again be surprised that you are tested. Some think it so strange that they should be tried. It would be strange if they were not tried. A Christian without trials would be, indeed, a strange Christian. Christian experience grows fat feeding on trials. You may as well try to rear a child without food as to gain an experience without trials. Caleb and Joshua understood this when they told the children of Israel that the trials they must meet were "bread" for them. Well, then, "beloved, think it not strange concerning the fiery trial which is to try you, as though some strange thing happened unto you; but rejoice, inasmuch as ye are partakers of Christ's sufferings; that, when his glory shall be revealed, ye may be glad also with exceeding joy" (I Pet. 4:12, 13).

Another great reason for rejoicing in tribulation is found in the fact that the Lord has full charge of training us through trial. Did you think the devil had control of your trials? If you did, you are greatly mistaken. All our trials come from the Lord. But does not the Bible say that God tempteth no man? Certainly it does, but there is a wide difference between temptation and trial. Satan tempts to tear down and destroy. The Lord tries us to build us up and make us strong.

Some of Satan's *temptations* are allowed to come to us to try us. Only those temptations are allowed to come to us as *trials* which the Lord sees are needed as trials to strengthen us. The Lord stands between us and the temptations of Satan, and tests each temptation, and only permits those to pass Him and come to us which will be beneficial as *trials* to strengthen our faith. If we are walking in the light, no temptation will ever come to us from Satan, which has not first been carefully inspected and measured by Him who "knoweth our frame" and "remembereth that we are dust," and who knows whether He can strengthen us to bear it and thereby build us up.

All this being true, how dare we murmur at any trial that ever comes to us? If we murmur, against whom shall we murmur? Since all our trials are permitted of the Lord, it follows that if we do any murmuring, we must murmur against the Lord. But if we are unwilling to murmur against Him, then *all* murmuring must cease forever. All murmuring against members of the family, against members of the church, against neighbors, or against anyone else on earth, living or dead, must cease forever. and all our murmurings must be made at the throne of God from whence all our trials come. Here is positive proof that all this is so. Paul, writing to the Corinthians, warns against murmuring like the Israelites who were destroyed, and then adds: "There hath no temptation taken you but such as is common to man; but God is faithful, who will not suffer you to be tempted above that ye are able; but will with the temptation also make a way to escape, that ye may be able to bear it" (I Cor. 10:13).

It was the Lord who led Israel to the Red Sea where they were walled in by the mountains. It was the Lord who permitted the Egyptian army to close up the trap and leave no human possibility of escape. God led the Israelites into this trial to strengthen their faith and give them an experience.

Up to the Red Sea experience they had walked by sight. God had first wrought the miracle before asking them to believe; but "we walk by faith, not by sight." And he who has not learned to trust God when he cannot understand how he is to be delivered has no enduring experience. The Israelites murmured because they could not see their way clear. They thought that some strange thing had happened to them and did not understand that God was giving them a trial to teach them to trust Him, and consequently they murmured against God. After they had failed to get the needed experience out of this trial, the Lord tried them again. He led them into the wilderness where there was no water fit to drink. The Lord knew that the water was bitter. The Lord knew that they were thirsty. The Lord led them there because He wanted them there. The Lord led them to this place to teach them to trust Him in a trial which they could not understand. They did not see that the Lord had led them into this trial to deepen their experience. They thought another strange thing had happened to them, hence they murmured again. The Lord continued to give them trials through which they were to become partakers of His holiness; but most of them continued to complain of the trials until their carcases fell in the wilderness.

Reader, all these things were written to save you from thinking it strange concerning the fiery trials which are to try you, as though some strange thing had happened unto you. "Now all these things happened unto them for ensamples; and they are *written for our admonition, upon whom the ends of the world are come*" (I Cor. 10:11).

Let us therefore *be admonished* by the fatal mistake of the murmuring Israelites, and expect that we shall be brought to Red Seas of difficulty and bitter waters of trial. And when there, we are not to think it strange concerning the fiery trials which are to try us, as though some strange thing happened unto us, but rejoice inasmuch as we are partakers of Christ's suffering.

The Lord knows how vital to Christian life and growth trials are, and how natural it would be to regard them as strange, and consequently to murmur at them; hence the Lord has plainly and positively stated that it is He himself who chastises, and that it is an experience "whereof all are partakers" "that we might be partakers of his holiness" (Heb. 12:5–13). Now, beloved, forever remember that you must be tried, and forever remember that the Lord himself has complete control of the trials which are to try you, and that He "*will not* suffer you to be tempted above that ye are able; but will with the temptation also make a way to escape, that ye may be able to bear it" (I Cor. 10:13). If you will remember this truth, your hands will no longer hang down with discouragement, nor your knees tremble with weakness, nor your path be crooked with failure.

In writing this I am not writing theory. I am writing *life*. These things are a part of my life, a part of my experience. I write them for the salvation of others because they have become my salvation.

From letters received, I quote two witnesses to the truth that one may glory in tribulation:

"Christ is all in all. I praise Him continually for what He is doing in my heart, and not only that, but for what He does for others. The way is not always easy, but, praise the Lord, He is ever a present help in time of need. My courage is good in the Lord. Praise the Lord for His Spirit that keeps me at all times! Praise the Lord, the anchor still holds!"

*   *   *   *   *

"Praise God, the anchor holds! Today I especially praise God for His keeping power. Thus far He has kept me from falling; and I know He will keep me in the future because He has said He would, and I am standing on His promises. I praise God for temptations, for I become stronger with every temptation."

CHAPTER SIXTEEN

ANOTHER REASON FOR REJOICING
IN TRIBULATION

There is still another reason for rejoicing in tribulation, which is the chief of all reasons. It is the reason which produces the highest type of rejoicing; it is the joy of heaven. Reader, would you not be satisfied with the joy that makes heaven rejoice? It is a reason for rejoicing from which all selfishness is separated. Here is the reason:

"Blessed be God, even the Father of our Lord Jesus Christ, the Father of mercies, and the God of all comfort; who comforteth us in all our tribulation, that we may be able to comfort them which are in any trouble, by the comfort wherewith we ourselves are comforted of God. For as the sufferings of Christ abound in us, so our consolation also aboundeth by Christ" (II Cor. 1:3–5).

There is no joy so great as bringing comfort to the comfortless. It is the joy that brought Christ to earth. In announcing His mission He read this: "The Spirit of the Lord God is upon me; because the Lord hath anointed me to preach good tidings unto the meek; he hath sent me to bind up the brokenhearted, to proclaim liberty to the captives, and the opening of the prison to them that are bound; ... to comfort all that mourn" (Isa. 61:1, 2). It was this joy that encouraged the Lord along the path of suffering. "For the joy that was set before him," He "endured the cross, despising the shame" (Heb. 12:2).

Reader, were you ever instrumental in bringing comfort to a sorrowing heart? Were you ever used of the Lord to lift the burden of the guilt of sin from a heart that was being crushed in despair? If so, you shared in the joy of heaven. "I say unto you, that likewise joy shall be in heaven over one sinner that repenteth, more than over ninety and nine just persons, which need no repentance" (Luke 15:7). Did you ever see the shadow of a great secret sorrow driven from the face of a sinning man or woman by the bright beams of the Sun of Righteousness as He arose with healing in His wings? Have you ever been used of the Lord to bring hope and strength and victory to a discouraged, defeated, despairing daughter of the Most High? Have you ever delivered a bruised, beaten, backslidden brother from the bondage of sin and death? If you are a stranger to all this, then there is a joy unspeakable that you may yet enjoy. But you can never share it until you have obtained an experience which will enable you to testify from personal experience that God can do all this for the chief of sinners.

And now since you are able to comfort others in their trouble only so far as you have experienced the fiery trials yourself, and come forth from them more than conqueror through Him that loved us, why should you think it strange concerning the fiery trials which are to try you, as though some strange thing had happened unto you? Why not rejoice that you are a partaker of Christ's sufferings, that you may be a partaker of His glory, which is none other than to bind up the brokenhearted, to proclaim liberty to the captives, and the comforting of all that mourn? Why should you murmur when you are tried when you know only so far as you have been tried and comforted are you able to comfort them that are in any trouble?

I want to witness here to the power of this truth in my own life. When it entered my heart, it brought a new joy and a new power to endure temptation. For the joy that is set before me of being better able to comfort all that mourn, I endure the cross, despising the shame, knowing that as the sufferings of Christ abound in me, so my consolation also abounds in Christ. When tempted to depart from the path of holiness, there passes before me the sinning, sorrowing multitude for which I will have no word of hope, no comforting message, if I fall under sin. For unless I am kept from falling, I shall be unable to tell others of His keeping power, for I am unable to tell with power any truth of the Word which is not made flesh, which has not become a part of my life. The life is "the light of men."

When I compare the enjoyment of sin for a season with the eternal, unspeakable joy of binding up the brokenhearted and comforting all that mourn, I say, "How can I sell such a birthright for a mess of potage?"

Reader, can you not, and will you not from this time, rejoice in tribulation, knowing that tribulation worketh patience, patience experience, and experience hope, a hope that you will not be ashamed of, but will tell for the comfort and salvation of a sinning, sorrowing, suffering world? Forever remember, when you are in trial, that the trial is not only for your good that you may be a partaker of His holiness, but that you are suffering for the salvation of the whole sinning world; you are suffering trial that you may obtain an experience which you can tell for the salvation of sinning men.

Therefore look beyond your own salvation while suffering affliction. Look, like Jesus, to the joy set before you of seeing others saved through your witness that the Lord is able to save to the uttermost. Forever remember that "as the sufferings of Christ abound in us, so our consolation also aboundeth by Christ" (II Cor. 1:5).

CHAPTER SEVENTEEN

FIRST A HOLY CHURCH,
THEN THE HOLY GHOST

The Holy Spirit, in His office of witness as manifested on the day of Pentecost, belongs to, and is given
to, the *church*. As lungs to breathing, so is the church
to the Holy Ghost. It is true that it is the globule, or
lung-cell, which receives the air; but God "fitly joined
together and compacted" these individual cells into
lungs before He breathed into them the breath of life;
and thus fitly joined together, these cells perform a
function which they could not perform separated. It is
also true that the Holy Ghost is given to "each one" as
on the day of Pentecost; but all must be of "one
accord," or "fitly joined together" in one body as was
the church then, with the Achans and Judases cleansed
out, before they can manifest the fulness of the witnessing power which God has given to the *church*.

The *church* is the "habitation of God through the
Spirit"; or, in other words, God inhabits the *church* by
means of His representative, the Holy Spirit. The individual members are all "fitly framed together" into

"an holy temple" "for an habitation of God through the Spirit" (Eph. 2:21, 22). And the gifts of the Spirit, which are the *demonstration* of the *power* of the Holy Spirit for service, for witnessing, are given to the *church*. "God hath set some in the *church*, first apostles, secondarily, prophets, thirdly teachers, after that miracles, then gifts of healings, helps, governments, diversities of tongues." All these are gifts of the Spirit, and God hath *set them in the church*. (I Cor. 12:28).

Some will admit all this but say that it is the *invisible* church, or body of Christ, to whom the fulness of the Holy Spirit is given; that, therefore, a visible or organized church is not necessary. But this is a mistake. It was a *visible, organized* church which received the power from on high on the day of Pentecost. It was a church which *Christ* had organized, but it was nevertheless *organized* and *visible*. Christ said, "The gates of hell shall not prevail against" "my church"; and He shows the church to be a visible, responsible body, which can hear of the trespassing of obstinate members and speak authoritatively to such members. (Matt. 18:15–18).

The writer is positive that he is able to point out the church that God will use to manifest forth the fulness of His power. Reader, are you anxious to find that church? Here is a description of it:

"And unto the angel of the church of the Laodiceans write: These things saith the Amen, the faithful and true witness, the beginning of the creation of God; I know thy works, that thou are neither cold nor hot; I would thou wert cold or hot. So then because thou art lukewarm, and neither cold nor hot, I will spew thee out of my mouth. Because thou sayest, I am rich, and increased with goods, and have need of nothing; and knowest not that thou art wretched, and miserable, and poor, and blind, and naked" (Rev. 3:14–17).

Reader, can you find the church described by this Scripture? Do you know of a church that has a form of godliness without the power? Do you know of a church that is proud and worldly while claiming to be the true church of God? Is this church your church? Do you reply that you don't know of a church that is not in that condition? It isn't enough to be able to find such a church; that is easy. But can you find a church in that condition that will *confess that they are in that condition?*—not a church that has a *few* members in it "that sigh and cry for all the abominations that be done in the midst thereof," but a whole church that will acknowledge that they are in that condition? Until such a church is found or formed, it will be impossible for God to manifest to the world the *fulness* of the power from on high.

When a church can be found that will acknowledge that they are wretched, and miserable, and poor, and blind, and naked, and will heed the exhortation that follows, then we shall have found the church through whom God will manifest all the power of the Holy Ghost. "I counsel thee to buy of me gold tried in the fire, that thou mayest be rich; and white raiment, that thou mayest be clothed, and that the shame of thy nakedness do not appear; and anoint thine eyes with eyesalve, that thou mayest see. As many as I love, I rebuke and chasten; be zealous therefore, and repent. Behold, I stand at the door, and knock; if any man hear my voice, and open the door, I will come in to him, and will sup with him, and he with me" (Rev. 3:18–20).

The church that will accept this fearful rebuke, repent, and open the door to Jesus Christ in the person of the Holy Spirit, will have all its denominational pride cleansed away. And it is this pride which, as much as any other sin, is keeping the Holy Ghost from the church.

From this we must deduct the solemn truth that we cannot have a church of apostolic power until we have a church of apostolic purity. A church must be *found* or *framed* out of which all the Achans and Ananiases have been cleansed.

If one Achan drove the power of God from "the church in the wilderness," many Achans will surely keep the "power from on high" away from the church of today. What, then, shall be done? Shall we cease to seek God for the baptism with His Spirit because His fulness cannot be realized until the church is cleansed? God forbid. First seek the Lord for His Spirit to cleanse you and then to use you to witness against the uncleanness of the church. By this means you will either cleanse the church or hear a call from the Spirit, saying, "Come out of her, my people, that ye be not partakers of her sins, and that ye receive not of her plagues."

CHAPTER EIGHTEEN

A SPIRIT-FILLED MEMBER POSSIBLE BEFORE A SPIRIT-FILLED CHURCH

While it is true that the *fulness* of the Spirit in the manifestation of all the gifts of the Spirit cannot be realized until the body of Christ, the church, will put away sin and make room for that fulness; yet you, dear reader, as a Christian individual, may even now be filled with the Spirit. You need not wait until the whole church is clean before you can be clean, neither need you wait until the whole church is filled before you can be filled. But it is one thing to be *filled* with the Spirit, and it is quite another thing to *manifest all* the *gifts* of the Spirit. There are some of the gifts of the Spirit that cannot appear while the church is filled with pride and unbelief; but there are other gifts that can.

The first manifestation of the Holy Ghost is to convince of sin. And if you are clean, or willing to be cleansed, from all the sins which fill the church, God will fill you with His Spirit, and make you a mighty witness against sin.

The gift of prophecy can be manifested in the church, and sin be mightily rebuked, while the manifestation of the fulness of the Spirit in miracles of healing may be withheld. Our Saviour cites an example in the following words: "Many lepers were in Israel in the time of Eliseus the prophet; and none of them was cleansed, saving Naaman the Syrian" (Luke 4:27). Thus it is plain that a prophet may be present in the church on whom the mantle of Elijah has fallen with a double portion of his spirit, and that prophet, under the influence of the Spirit, may mightily rebuke sin, and at the same time the manifestation of the gifts of healing may be withheld from the "many lepers" in the church.

Now these things are written to remove the impression, so general, that as soon as one is filled with the Spirit, he will immediately speak with tongues, or open the eyes of the blind, or perform some other mighty miracle of healing. There are many who are waiting for these signs to appear before they will believe that they can be filled with the Spirit. John the Baptist was "filled with the Holy Ghost" from his birth (Luke 1:15), and yet it is written, "John did no miracle."

And here is manifested the mercy of God. A sin-filled church is not prepared for mighty miracles of healing unless a previous work can be accomplished for them; for the mighty miracles would only lead the church to commit the unpardonable sin.

CHAPTER NINETEEN

MIRACLES AND THE SIN AGAINST THE HOLY GHOST

The men who rejected John's message of repentance were among those who committed the unpardonable sin when "Jesus, being full of the Holy Ghost"—the same power which filled John—revealed other manifestations of the Spirit and wrought mighty miracles of healing. It was over the *miracles* of healing wrought by our Lord that the leaders in the church committed the unpardonable sin. By these miracles they were compelled to take a position. They had tried to maintain a neutral position in regard to John's message. They neither repented of their sins nor openly denounced him. But now that they were in the presence of the miracles of Christ, and the people were deserting them to follow Jesus, they were compelled to take a position. But. not having walked in the light when the Holy Ghost through John called to repentance, they were wholly unprepared to discern the source of the miracles when the Holy Ghost through Jesus opened the eyes of the blind and cast out devils. Hence they declared that the miracles were wrought "by Beelzebub, the prince of the devils" (Matt. 12:24).

In thus speaking against the manifestation of the Holy Ghost, they rejected the final and only remaining effort that God could make for their salvation—the manifestation of the Holy Ghost; and they cut themselves off from salvation. If I refuse as poison the only remedy that can heal me, I have committed the unpardonable sin against my life, and I must die. So when the Jews rejected as devilish the full and final display of the power of the Holy Spirit to save them from sin and death, they committed the unpardonable sin and must perish in their sins.

Thus it is plain that one may be filled with the Spirit, and witness in the power of the Spirit against sin, before the manifestation of the Spirit in miracles of healing appears.

Is it not also clear, dear reader, that you may be filled to do a work in the backslidden church before that church is prepared for the miracle-working of the Spirit if the church is to be saved from the awful fate of committing the sin against the Holy Ghost?

Is it not also clear, dear reader, that you may be filled with the Spirit, and witness with power for righteousness against sin, before the other manifestations of the Spirit in the gift of tongues and miracles of healing shall appear? Let us therefore continue to study how we may be filled with the Spirit and become a burning and shining light.

It is possible for you to be so filled with the Spirit as to burn so warmly and shine so brightly as to cause the sinners in Zion to get right, or to get out, or to get you out. In any case the result will be a blessing. There will be a separation from sin. Backslidden Israel continued to drive the Spirit-filled prophets out of the church until they drove Christ to Calvary; and then of those who had been driven out of the synagogues, He organized a new church, filled with the new wine of the kingdom, from which church the Holy Ghost was able to drive out hypocrites and keep them out. God will have a clean church, whether it be one cleansed out as the result of confession or called out as the result of oppression. And the Lord wants you to be filled with the Spirit and begin now to burn and to shine.

CHAPTER TWENTY

FILLING AND FEELING

Now that it is plain that the Lord wants to fill you with His Spirit, and that you need not wait for the whole church to be filled, let us come directly to the vital question of receiving.

Bear in mind that you are now seeking the baptism with the Holy Ghost for *service*, not for self. When by the Spirit you were born again, you received a blessing primarily for yourself, for your own needs. And when the Spirit wrought in you to continue that new life and build up a character by mortifying the deeds of the body and giving you continual victory, this, too, was an operation of the Spirit for your own needs. You needed all this, first of all, for your own salvation; and second, as an experience through which you have a hope of salvation that you are not ashamed of, and not ashamed to tell. For certainly he who is not born of the Spirit is not prepared to witness for the Lord, nor is he who is not built up and upheld by the Spirit qualified to witness for Him. He has nothing to witness, nothing to tell.

Thus we see that the work of the Spirit in conversion and in character-building is primarily for our own salvation and secondly for the salvation of others; but the baptism with the Spirit is *primarily* for service for the salvation of others.

Of our Saviour's baptism with the Holy Ghost it is written, "God anointed Jesus of Nazareth with the Holy Ghost and with *power;* who went about *doing good.*" This anointing was not primarily for His own needs, not to enable Him to go about and *be* good, for He had been good all His life, but that He might go about *"doing good."*

When the disciples were baptized on the day of Pentecost, the Holy Ghost came not to convict them of sin. This the Spirit had already done. They did not spend the day in settling old grudges, for this had been accomplished, if not before, at least in the ten days during which "all continued with one accord in prayer and supplication" (Acts 1:14). So that the Holy Ghost did not come to *convince* them of *sin,* but to *qualify* them for *service.* "And they were all filled with the Holy Ghost, and began *to speak*" (Acts 2:4). They did not supplicate for forgiveness, nor make confession one to another, but they *began to speak* to the amazed multitude.

Now that it is clear that you are to seek the baptism with the Holy Ghost for *service* in the salvation of sinners, when and where do you expect to experience that power?

Jesus was anointed with the Holy Ghost and with power at the river Jordan, but there was no visible manifestation of power at that time. There was the appearance of a dove, but a dove is not a symbol of power. He was anointed with the Holy Ghost and with power that He might go about doing good, but that power was not manifest until He "went about doing good."

On the day of Pentecost the disciples were baptized with power, and the accompanying manifestations of power were not to *convince* them that they were baptized, but to *qualify* them for the *work of that very hour*. They did not spend the day in *feeling;* they spent the day in *working*.

So we have not the *feelings* of the apostles, but the *acts* of the apostles. We have no record of how John or Christ or the disciples *felt* when they were baptized, but we do have a record of what they *did* when they were baptized. None of the disciples ever refer to how they felt or how they looked, and we believe that they were as oblivious of the personal effect of the baptism as was Moses after he came forth from his baptism in the flaming glory of Sinai. Of him it is written, "And when Aaron and all the children of Israel saw Moses, behold, the skin of his face shone; and they were afraid to come nigh him." But "Moses wist not that the skin of his face shone" (Ex. 34:29, 30).

All this is written to show that the baptism with the Holy Ghost is for practical service and not for physical sensation. Whatever there be of the manifestation of tongues of fire or shining faces, these are not so much for the benefit of the shining saint as for the sinning multitude.

There has been much noisy demonstration among a class who seem to think that the baptism with the Holy Ghost is primarily for the benefit of the receiver, to be enjoyed amid noisy demonstrations of feeling. But the threshing machine is not run to make the threshing machine feel good, but to thresh out the grain. When I was a farmer boy, I noticed that the threshing machine running empty made more noise than when filled. I noticed that when the "feeder" ran out of grain, the driver hastened to halt the horses. The power was for threshing the wheat, not for shaking the machine. I noticed when the machine was at work, the deafening rattle of empty machinery softened into a subdued song of service.

The trouble with some of the teaching and practice on this important theme is that its advocates seem to think that the power was intended more for the machine than for the grain; consequently there has been much of what might be termed "running empty." Power is never applied to threshing machines except for threshing purposes, and in like manner power for service is never applied by the great Master-builder to His servants except when they are ready to serve and there is someone to serve. Don't ask the Lord to turn on the power and rattle the machinery to prove to you that the Lord will do what He has promised.

But should we not wait for the sound of a mighty rushing wind or the sight of cloven tongues of fire? We should no more demand a second Pentecost to prove that the Holy Spirit is ours than we should demand a second Calvary before believing that salvation from sin

is ours. Just as "once in the end of the world" "He appeared to put away sin by the sacrifice of himself," so
once "in the last days" did the Lord fulfil His promise
to pour out His Spirit "upon all flesh." And just as all
men in all time can come and be cleansed in the blood
of the fountain opened for sin and uncleanness "by
Christ *crucified*," just so they can come and be filled
with the living waters poured out on Pentecost by
Christ *glorified*. "In the last day, that great day of the
feast, Jesus stood and cried, saying, If any man thirst,
let him come unto me, and drink. He that believeth on
me, as the scripture hath said, out of his belly shall flow
rivers of living water. (But this spake he of the Spirit
which they that believe on him should receive; for the
Holy Ghost was not yet given, because that Jesus was
not yet glorified.)" (John 7:37–39).

And we should no more demand a repetition of the
earthquake of Calvary before we would be cleansed
with the blood than we should demand a repetition of
the rushing wind of Pentecost before we will be filled
with the Spirit.

CHAPTER TWENTY-ONE

THE SPIRIT CALLS FOR CONSECRATION

She was a young woman of a prominent family, who had followed her convictions of Christian life and labor through self-denial, suffering, and reproach. She was sorely afflicted with tuberculosis and a complication of diseases; but with her little remaining strength she labored to bless a sinning world in mansion, in mission, and in prison cell.

She hungered for more power for holy living and labor. She heard the message, "Receive ye the Holy Ghost," and earnestly sought the necessary cleansing. From faith to faith she followed on to know the Lord until her mind became exercised concerning healing. She was instructed to continue to pray and study the Scripture promises concerning healing, and if faith came, to call for the elders.

Later she called for prayer, and an hour was appointed for the solemn service. The doctor had the day before declared that her lungs were badly affected with tuberculosis. When the hour arrived and all was in readiness, one minister started to ask her the question,

"Now, sister, if the Lord does not heal you, will the disappointment drive you into discouragement?" She stopped the minister in the middle of the question and said in calm confidence, "Don't say 'if'; the Lord will heal me." Those present quickly perceived that she had faith to be healed, and without further delay they knelt to pray for healing. Only a few sentences of prayer had been offered when the Spirit of God came upon her, and for four hours she was under His control. During this time there was accomplished a marvelous work of healing, pruning, and consecration. The healing power of God was remarkably perceptible as it moved from one diseased organ to another, accomplishing a most wonderful work of healing which, from my personal knowledge, has been permanent ever since. The recipient of the great blessing poured out her restored life and ever-springing health in a ceaseless ministry of loving labor for the unrighteous and unlovely.

But it is not for the marvelous manifestation of healing and filling by the Holy Ghost that this witness is introduced here, but for the *faith* which brought it and the *cleansing* and *consecration* that accompanied it. Oh, that every reader of this could have witnessed the displeasure manifested by the Spirit on this occasion against all conformity to the world in the wearing of gold or display in dress. When this part of the experience was over, our sister did not possess a hat or dress plain enough to meet her enlightened views on the plainness and simplicity of dress.

Now followed a most touching and impressive experience. After lying quiet for a time, the young woman was heard to say in confiding, whispered tones,

"Anywhere, anywhere, everywhere." Several times these words were repeated, each time with louder tones and added emphasis. When, later, the meaning of these words was explained, it was learned that after she was healed and pruned, the Lord tested her love and willingness to labor for Him anywhere and every-where by presenting before her mind in quick succession the dark outline maps of Mexico, South America, and South Africa.

Oh, how much it means to surrender all to God, and pray for the healing or the baptism with the Holy Spirit! Many would like to receive power from on high if only they could *manage* that power. But let it be understood once and forever that he who seeks to be filled with the Holy Ghost, must yield unqualified obedience to the teaching and directing of the Spirit.

He may never be led beyond the neighborhood work of a humble home, but there must be a willing-ness to be anything or do anything or to go anywhere or nowhere as the Lord may lead. Paul preferred to wit-ness in Jerusalem and work for the Jews, but the Lord wanted him to go "far hence unto the Gentiles," and to the Gentiles he went. In later years he and his com-pany wanted to preach in Asia, but "were forbidden of the Holy Ghost to preach the word in Asia," and when they essayed to go into Bithynia, "the Spirit suffered them not." "And after he had seen the vision, immediately we endeavored to go into Macedonia, assuredly gathering that the Lord had called us for to preach the gospel unto them."

But the Spirit that ever leads never *leaves*. "I will pray the Father, and he shall give you another Comforter, that he may abide with you *forever*"; and there is "peace and joy in the Holy Ghost," whether it be in palace or prison, native land or darkest Africa. He who is "walking in the fear of the Lord, and in the comfort of the Holy Ghost" can walk into prison or jungle amid pain and pestilence and still rejoice in the "peace and joy in the Holy Ghost."

Oh, the blessedness of complete surrender! Oh, the light and joy in the leading of the Spirit! Reader, surrender and let Him lead you.

> There's a night in self-assertion
>   Like the night of Egypt's wrath,
> But the sunshine of surrender
>   Sheds a light o'er all the path.
> There's a strife on self-assertion
>   Like the storm-tossed breakers' crest;
> There's a peace in consecration
>   Like a waveless ocean's rest.

CHAPTER TWENTY-TWO

"THE PROMISE OF THE SPIRIT"

"Christ hath redeemed us from the curse of the law, being made a curse for us; . . . that the blessing of Abraham might come on the Gentiles through Jesus Christ, *that we might receive the promise of the Spirit through faith.*"

How, then, shall I know that I have received the power from on high for witnessing if I am not to base my belief on some physical sensation? If I am not to feel that I am filled before I am to believe I am filled, how am I to *know* that I am filled? What do you want me to do? And what do you mean by "receive ye the Holy Ghost"? What constitutes receiving the Holy Ghost? Will there be any difference in my life and labor after I receive the Holy Ghost than before? I don't want to be presumptuous; I don't want to deceive myself. These are some of the thoughts which come rushing into the mind at this point.

How did you learn that your sins were forgiven? Did you accept it by faith or by sight? Do you base your faith that you are forgiven on some physical sight. or do you base it on the naked Word of God? If you have not learned to "walk by faith, not by sight," you will have to learn it before you can "receive the promise of the Spirit *through faith.*" If your belief rests on signs and wonders, you are yet in the kindergarten class. You are still a babe in Christ. Christ said to doubting Thomas, "Thomas, because thou hast seen me, thou hast believed; blessed are they that have not seen, and yet have believed" (John 20:29).

God will receive babes into a kindergarten class, and teach them with visible blocks and sticks; but He wants them to hasten to graduate out of the kindergarten class of signs and sight into the first reader of faith. When the Israelites left Egypt, they were a great kindergarten class, and the work of the Lord in teaching them for forty years was to get them to believe His *Word before* they saw the wonders. But few of them ever entered the first grade of faith. "So we see that they could not enter in because of unbelief."

An old man of eighty years, who had been recently converted, arose in a revival meeting and, with face beaming with joy, told how the Lord had pardoned all his sins; how he had lived a profane, wicked life for seventy-nine years, and how the Lord had, at the eleventh hour, forgiven all his sins. And then he gave his proof. He said when he saw himself a sinner, and that he had sinned so long, it seemed impossible to believe that the Lord would pardon so great a sinner, so he asked the Lord to show him a sign; that if he was really forgiven, the Lord would remove a large wen above his temple. With moistened eyes he declared that the Lord had done it, and pointed to the scar as proof. And with a burst of joy he declared his thankfulness to God. I did not hesitate to rejoice with him, for I said to myself, "He is only a babe in Christ. He is in the kindergarten class. But the time will come when the Lord will ask him to believe without a sign; when He will call on him to transfer his faith from the root of a wen to the rock of His Word."

Reader, how did you gain the victory over that besetting sin? If you haven't the victory, you are not yet prepared for the reception of the Spirit for witnessing, for you have nothing worth telling. If you have the victory, how did you obtain it? Did you not go to the Lord in your weakness and acknowledge your sins and ask Him to keep you from falling? Did you not then accept His promise to keep you before you saw any sign that you were kept? Did you not accept the forgiveness of your sins because the Lord in His Word promised that "if we confess our sins, he is faithful and just to forgive us our sins, and to cleanse us from all unrighteousness"? (I John 1:9). Did you not base your faith on His promise rather than on your feelings? Did you not accept the keeping power because the Lord in His Word says, "God is faithful, who will not suffer you to be tempted above that ye are able, but will with the temptation also make a way to escape, that ye may be able to bear it"? (I Cor. 10:13). Did you not base your faith on His promise rather than on your feelings? Was not your joy on being forgiven and kept the *result* of believing rather than your believing the result of your joy? "Now the God of hope fill you with all joy and peace *in believing*" (Rom. 15:13).

Can you not see that peace and joy and all other promised blessings come to us *"in believing,"* not in our unbelief? If God should grant peace and joy before we believed, while we were still in unbelief, it would make us peaceful and joyful unbelievers. But peace and joy are not for those still in unbelief. They are for the believers. They are the *fruits* of the *Spirit already received by faith*, not material out of which faith for receiving the Spirit is made.

And again, if you were filled with the Spirit *before* you received the *promise by faith*, would you not be a Spirit-filled unbeliever? Can you not see that the Spirit for service must come in response to faith just as forgiveness or victory over temptation came in response to faith?

Should a sinner come to you and ask the way to forgiveness of sin, would you not point him to the promise and ask him to believe it even *before* he *felt* he was forgiven? And if he came again under great temptation, would you not point him to the promise and ask him to accept deliverance *by faith, before he felt the deliverance?*

Now that you are seeking to be filled with the Spirit that you may serve as a powerful witness for God, do you not think you had better take your own treatment? Should you not believe God's promise to fill you before you demand to see the signs which follow a Spirit-filled life?

"We walk by faith, not by sight." And that means all the way. Reader, when you are called upon to walk a step farther in the path of faith, will you not take that step by faith?

"Without faith it is impossible to please God."

"All eternity will not be too long," writes a correspondent, "for me to praise Him for the mighty and wonderful deliverance wrought in my life since the first Sabbath you talked to us here. I think it was March 25, and having that day received indubitable evidence that I had been born into the kingdom of God, I shall henceforth regard it as my spiritual birthday.

"I now realize what is meant by the 'obedience of faith.' It is not worked out by my own will-power. It is the result of taking each promise of God as an actual fulfilment. In the exercise of this new kind of obedience, new for me, at any rate, I am continually coming off more than conqueror over my besetments. In these conflicts I am the engine of war, but the force impelling it flows from the Source of everlasting strength.

"Truly in my case the Lord has been changing each weakness into power; and in all truth and soberness, my brother, I say, *I know* that of all professing the name of Christ with whom I have ever been brought into contact, I have been the weakest of the weak. Now, however, day by day, this condition is changing radically, and I am becoming 'strong in the Lord, and in the power of his might.' The citadel of my heart is now in the possession of the Holy Spirit, and Satan is at last outside its walls. Jesus knocks no longer for admission. He is inside already. The tables are now turned, and Satan stands without and knocks, but, glory to the cross of Calvary, let him knock in vain forever! The language of earth is inadequate to give

vent to my joy and sense of freedom—the glorious
liberty of the children of God! And being Christ's free-
man, who dare make me a slave again?"

CHAPTER TWENTY-THREE

HOW TO FIND FAITH

Since it is *by faith* that we receive the promise of the Spirit, and since "faith cometh by hearing, and hearing by the word of God," the only way to get sufficient faith to grasp the promise of the Spirit, is to hear what the Word of God promises concerning the Spirit.

In the first place, the Word of God says: "Know ye not that your body is the temple of the Holy Ghost which is in you, which ye have of God, and ye are not your own? For ye are bought with a price; therefore glorify God in your body, and in your spirit, which are God's" (I Cor. 6:19, 20).

The life which you now have is of God. And the very fact that you are kept alive by the Spirit of God is evidence of God's love. Were it not for the sacrifice of Christ, the wages of sin, which is death, would long since have been demanded. But the Lord desires that we shall have more than what we term natural life, and more than a new existence in the spiritual life. Says Christ, "I am come that they might have life, and that they might have it *more abundantly*" (John 10:10). It is the more abundant life that we are now seeking. It is the overflow of life; it is the outflow of the "rivers of living water" we are searching for (John 7:37–39).

Remember the Word of God says that "ye are bought with a price," that "ye are not your own." Remember also that the same Word says that "*your body is the temple of the Holy Ghost.*" Therefore *your body was bought for the very purpose of being a temple of the Holy Ghost.* Therefore, if you do not have that more abundant life, that filling of the Spirit, that overflowing fountain of life, the plan of God concerning you has not been met. For He bought you for a wellspring of His Spirit.

Let us illustrate by a conversation between the governor of a great state and his aristocratic neighbor.

Neighbor: Governor, I hear you have purchased that old rookery at the corner of Twenty-first Street and Broadway. What are you going to do with it? Are you going to start a hennery?

Governor: No, neighbor, I am going to *live* in that house.

Neighbor: What, *live* in that house! Don't you know that that house is swarming with vermin from cellar to garret?

Governor: Yes, I know it, but I will destroy the vermin.

Neighbor: But, Governor, you cannot mean that you are really going to live in that old rookery. Don't you know that the walls are all disfigured with obscene pictures?

Governor: Yes, I looked them all over. But I will erase the indecent pictures and embellish its walls with pictures of virtue and beauty.

Neighbor: Now, Governor, I must be plain with you: that house is a house of ill-fame; and if you move into it, it will cost you your reputation.

Governor: I knew all that and more when I bought it. But it will not be a house of ill-fame when I move into it. By living an honorable life in that house, I shall give it a new reputation. That house was the home of my noble father; but it fell into wicked hands and lost its good name; but I, his son, have purchased that old residence on purpose to live in it and redeem its good name. I am not afraid of losing my reputation. Only its tarnished reputation will suffer. I have sufficient reputation among the good people of my state, as an upright man, to restore to the old homestead an honorable name.

Reader, you will find this truth told in Titus 3:1–6. It was not because of the works of righteousness which we had done that we received the renewing of the Holy Ghost. The Lord purchased us after a thorough inspection. He purchased us to live in us by His Holy Spirit after beholding all the ruin that sin had made. He has not been surprised at our sinfulness, but He has been pained that we would not submit to "the washing of regeneration, and renewing of the Holy Ghost."

Do not ever again think that the baptism with the Spirit is a kind of expensive extra, outside of the great plan of God for our salvation. This indwelling and outflowing promise of the Spirit is as much yours according to the plan of salvation as the forgiveness of sins. It hangs on the same stem of faith as all the other blessings—"He that believeth on me" (John 7:38, 39).

Now, dear reader, never again doubt the Lord's willingness to make you an overflowing fountain. If you want to see how anxious He is to dwell in you by His Spirit, go to Gethsemane and see your Saviour crushed to earth by the sin of the world, and hear Him cry, "If this cup may not pass away from me, except I drink it, thy will be done"; and remember that all this was paid for you that you might be filled with the Spirit. Hear Him again as, nailed to the cross, He cries, "My God, my God, why hast thou forsaken me?" And when the spear point pierces His side and He pours out the blood of a broken heart—remember that this was done that you might be filled with the Spirit. "Receive ye the Holy Ghost."

CHAPTER TWENTY-FOUR

THE HOLY GHOST, THE VICEGERENT

OF CHRIST

It is a night in Jerusalem, the saddest night since sin separated man from God. The city is thronged with worshippers from all the world. It is the feast of the Passover. The Lord and His disciples in the upper room have eaten the paschal lamb. The lamb of "that great day" has met the Lamb of God. Type has touched antitype. The Son of God, from the throne of the universe, has girded himself as a servant and, kneeling before sinful men, has bathed their feet with His own immaculate hands. He has eaten of the broken bread and drunk of the poured-out wine, the symbols of His suffering and death. Only a few minutes separate the scene of the upper room from the struggle of the garden. Only a few minutes now between the blood on the doorpost and the blood on the brow.

For a little while the Shepherd is with His sheep. Soon they will smite the Shepherd, and the sheep will be scattered. What momentous moments! Weighty, indeed, is every word spoken now.

He asks the traitor to hasten and retire, and when he is gone, He speaks thus:

"Little children, yet a little while I am with you. Ye shall seek me, and as I said unto the Jews, Whither I go, ye cannot come; so now I say to you."

Simon Peter: "Lord, whither goest thou?"

The Lord: "Whither I go, thou canst not follow me now; but thou shalt follow me afterwards."

Simon Peter: "Lord, why cannot I follow thee now? I will lay down my life for thy sake."

This announcement of His departure brings sorrow to the hearts of the disciples. They are troubled. They have never thought of being separated from Him. They have separated from honored Pharisees, from friends, and from family, from everything and from everybody, that they might be with their Lord. Now *He* is going away. Their hearts are troubled.

"Let not your hearts be troubled; ye believe in God, believe also in me. In my Father's house are many mansions; if it were not so, I would have told you. I go to prepare a place for you. And if I go and prepare a place for you, I will come again, and receive you unto myself; that where I am, there ye may be also."

Precious promise! blessed hope! But this does not heal the heartache. No promise of *mansions to come* can take the place of a *present Saviour*.

But what will we do when He is gone? It will be lonely when He is away, they think.

I was in a mission in New York. It was when the Klondike excitement was at its height. The leader of the meeting made reference to it, and exhorted his hearers to seek first the kingdom of God. A testimony meeting followed. One man said he had no home on Fifth Avenue, but that he had a home on high and hoped some day to see it. Another said he could not get to the Klondike to gather gold, but that the streets before his heavenly mansion were paved with gold, and he longed to behold their glittering glory. Another said his home was plainly furnished, but that his mansion on high was richly decorated, and he longed to see its polished floors and pictured walls.

Just then a man arose with labored effort. He was twitching in every muscle; he had sown to the flesh and was reaping a sad harvest of physical ruin. I pitied him and thought, "Why did not someone who knew him prevent him from bringing mortification to himself and to his hearers?" I could not endure to look at him. The sight was too painful. But as he spoke his muscles grew steady. When I turned to look at him again, his face flashed forth the light of heaven, and he said, "One year ago I was a poor drunkard, staggering from saloon to saloon, trading my lead pencils for rum. I was steeped in drink and sin; but while in that condition my Saviour found me and saved me from it all. And now you may talk of wanting to see your mansions on high with their costly furnishings and streets of gold, but I long to see the face of the Son of God who saved me and washed me clean in His own blood."

No promise of mansions will supply the place of that Saviour in the heart of the sinner whom He has saved from his sins.

> Oh, the joy of those mansions is Jesus
> Without Him they're barren and cold!
> Oh, the joy of those mansions is Jesus
> I hunger His face to behold!

The promise of mansions did not satisfy the mourning disciples. The mansions will be grand, but, oh, how lonesome while we wait! Who will take His place while we wait? Who will be with us and comfort us when He is gone?

"I will pray the Father, and he shall give you *another Comforter*, that he may abide with you forever; even the Spirit of truth; whom the world cannot receive, because it seeth him not, neither knoweth him; but ye know him; for he dwelleth with you, and shall be in you. I will not leave you comfortless; I will come to you" (John 14:16–18).

Glorious comfort! But still their hearts were troubled. Who would meet the cunning questions of the Pharisees? Oh, that we might remember the words of truth with which He met their subtle errors!

"The Comforter, which is the Holy Ghost, whom the Father will send in my name, he shall teach you all things, and bring all things to your remembrance, whatsoever I have said unto you" (John 14:26).

Blessed promise! But what shall we do with the sick and suffering? When fathers and mothers and brothers and sisters come bringing their sick and suffering and ask for the healing touch of the Master's hands, how shall we answer their pleading cries?

"Verily, verily, I say unto you, He that believeth on me, the works that I do shall he do also; and greater works than these shall he do, because I go unto the Father. And whatsoever ye shall ask in my name, that will I do, that the Father may be glorified in the Son. If ye shall ask anything in my name, that will I do. If ye love me, ye will keep my commandments" (John 14:12–15, R.V.).

Wonderful promise! But how shall we convince the world of sin in not believing on Him when He is gone? And how shall we convince them that He whom they cannot see is able to forgive sins and grant them righteousness? How shall we convince them of the final judgment and vindication of His cause over the prince of this world? Who will believe our testimony concerning the life and death and triumphant ascension to the right hand of God, of one whom they never saw and cannot see?

It does not seem to them expedient that He should go away where He could not appear as a living witness to all men, to confirm that which was taught concerning Him and His salvation. They could see no light in His going away, and their hearts were still filled with sorrow when He said:

"Because I have said these things unto you, sorrow hath filled your heart. Nevertheless I tell you the truth: It is expedient for you that I go away; for if I

go not away, the Comforter will not come unto you; but
if I depart, I will send him unto you. And when he is
come, he will convict [R.V.] the world of sin, and of
righteousness, and of judgment; of sin, because they
believe not on me; of righteousness, because I go to
my Father, and ye see me no more; of judgment, because the prince of this world is judged." "Ye shall receive power after that the Holy Ghost is come upon
you; and ye shall be witnesses unto me, both in Jerusalem and in all Judea, and in Samaria, and unto the
uttermost part of the earth" (John 16:6–11; Acts 1:8).

Reader, do you sometimes feel like an orphan in
this cold world? Do you wish that He who comforted
all that mourn were here as He was in the home of
Mary and Martha and Lazarus to bring comfort and
joy and healing to your life? Then receive ye the
Holy Ghost, that other Comforter. "I will pray the
Father, and he shall give you another Comforter, that
he may abide with you forever.... I will not leave
you comfortless; I will come to you."

Do you hunger for truth? Do you sometimes wish
you might sit at His feet and be taught the Scriptures
as Mary did in her home in Bethany? "Receive ye the
Holy Ghost." "When he the Spirit of truth, is come,
he will guide you into all truth. For he shall not speak
of himself; but whatsoever he shall hear, that shall he
speak; and he will show you things to come. He shall
glorify me; for he shall receive of mine, and shall show
it unto you" (John 16:13, 14).

Do you hunger for power to convict the world of
the sinfulness of sin, of the gift of righteousness, and

the final and glorious vindication of the Prince of Peace over the prince of this world? Then receive ye the promised power from on high, that other Comforter, for the Lord has promised that He shall do all this.

Let us illustrate by supposing a possible scene. It is the ninth day, the day before Pentecost. Peter and John have left the praying company for a few minutes and are walking pensively down the street to buy bread for their companions. Suddenly they confront a priest who recognizes them and addresses them thus:

"Well, well, if here isn't Peter and John. How glad I am to see you and to know that at last you are free from that awful delusion.

Peter: What delusion?

Priest: The delusion that the Nazarene was the Messiah.

Peter: What makes you think that we are free from that so-called delusion?

Priest: I should think you would be, now that He is dead.

Peter: Dead! no indeed, He isn't. He is resurrected and is alive forevermore.

Priest: Nonsense. He is dead, for I saw Him die. That resurrection story is a fraud. You, His deluded disciples, came by night and stole His body, and now circulate the lying report that He rose from the dead. This I hear from the most influential people in the church and state. Why continue the fraud? No one will believe your story.

Peter: Fraud! There is no fraud. He is risen. I saw Him, and ate with Him, and talked with Him, and so have we all. He is not only risen, but ascended to the right hand of God whence He came. I saw Him ascend. He is not dead. He is alive—alive forevermore.

Priest: Delusion upon delusion! Falsehood upon falsehood! Ascended—never! He is dead forevermore.

Peter: That is false. He is——

John: Peter, don't tarry here; let us hasten on. When we are alone, I will tell you what impresses me deeply. And this it is, Peter. We can make no impression upon the priest until the Holy Ghost is come. Rememberest thou not how He spake while He was yet with us, saying: "Tarry ye in the city of Jerusalem, until ye be endued with power from on high"? And, "Ye shall receive power, after that the Holy Ghost is come upon you; and ye shall be witnesses unto me." "Nevertheless I tell you the truth; It is expedient for you that I go away: for if I go not away, the Comforter will not come unto you; but if I depart, I will send him unto you. And when he is come, *he will convince the world of sin, and of righteousness, and of judgment; of sin, because they believe not on me; of righteousness, because I go to my Father, and ye see me no more;* of judgment, because the prince of this world is judged"?

Let us return to the upper room and wait for the promise of the Spirit. Did you not see how powerless you were to convict the priest? Oh, how helpless we are! Let us return and pray more earnestly for the promised power.

"And when the day of Pentecost was fully come, they were all with one accord in one place. And suddenly there came a sound from heaven as of a rushing mighty wind, and it filled all the house where they were sitting. And there appeared unto them cloven tongues like as of fire, and it sat upon each of them. And they were all filled with the Holy Ghost, and began to speak with other tongues, as the Spirit gave them utterance. . . . Now when this was noised abroad, the multitude came together, and were confounded, . . . and they were all amazed and marvelled" (Acts 2:1-7).

I can easily think of that stubborn priest hurrying with the surging multitude to the place of power. I can see him pressing his way through the eager crowd until he finds himself at the very feet of Peter who is just saying with a strange convincing power:

"Men and brethren, let me freely speak unto you of the patriarch David, that he is both dead and buried, and his sepulchre is with us unto this day. Therefore being a prophet, and knowing that God had sworn with an oath to him, that of the fruit of his loins, according to the flesh, he would raise up Christ to sit on his throne; he seeing this before spake of the resurrection of Christ, that his soul was not left in hell, neither his flesh did see corruption. This Jesus hath God raised up, whereof we all are witnesses. Therefore being by the right hand of God exalted, and having received of the Father the promise of the Holy Ghost, he hath shed forth this, which ye now see and hear. For David is not ascended into the heavens; but he saith himself, The Lord said unto my Lord, Sit thou on my right hand, until I make thy foes thy footstool. Therefore let all the house of Israel know assuredly, that God hath made that same Jesus, whom ye crucified, both Lord and Christ" (Acts 2: 29–36).

And now I see this same priest (for "a great company of the priests were obedient to the faith") listening, startled, silent, and subdued until Peter reaches this point; and then I hear him, pricked in his heart, with earnestness cry out, "Men and brethren, what shall we do?"

Reader, can you not see that what is needed today to silence the scoffer, to convict of sin and of righteousness, to prove the resurrection, and to point out Jesus at the right hand of God, is the Holy Ghost from on high?

Another promise to you that you may receive the gift of the Holy Ghost, the same power that moved the multitude on the morning of Pentecost, is found in Peter's answer, thus: "Repent, and be baptized every one of you in the name of Jesus Christ for the remission of sins, and *ye shall receive the gift of the Holy Ghost.* For the promise is unto you, and to your children, and to all that are afar off, even as many as the Lord our God shall call" (Acts 2:38, 39).

CHAPTER TWENTY-FIVE

THE HOLY GHOST A GIFT

Peter told the wicked men who had crucified Christ that if they would repent and be baptized in the name of Christ for the remission of sins, they, *even they*, should receive the *gift* of the Holy Ghost; receive that power which so mightily moved the multitude on that Pentecostal morning. But it must be received as a *gift*. Certainly those wicked men had not earned the greatest gift God can bestow. Neither could they earn the gift by repentance, nor by baptism.

Even repentance and forgiveness of sins—yes, from repentance to regeneration and the renewal of the Holy Ghost, all, *all* are gifts from God. "Him hath God exalted with his right hand to be a Prince and a Saviour, for to *give repentance* to Israel and *forgiveness of sins*" (Acts 5:31). "For by grace are ye saved through faith; and that not of yourselves; it is the *gift* of God; not of works, lest any man should boast" (Eph. 2:8, 9).

Reader, how did you come to repent? The Lord gave you repentance, did He? That is right. And you received it as a *gift?* You did not earn it, did you?

No, you received it wholly as a *gift*. How did you receive forgiveness of sins? The Lord gave it to you, did He? That is right too. And you simply asked for it and accepted it as a merciful gift from God. How did you obtain the victory over that strong temptation, that besetting sin? You received it as a *gift*, did you? Yes, "thanks be to God, which *giveth* us the *victory* through our Lord Jesus Christ."

Reader, don't you think that after receiving so many *gifts* from God, you ought to be accustomed to receiving gifts, so that you could receive the *gift* of the Holy Ghost?

Do not think of offering the Lord anything for this gift, for this would only show how little you appreciated the gift. In the first place, you have nothing to give. You yourself belong to God. "Ye are not your own; for ye are bought with a price; therefore glorify God in your body, and in your spirit, which are God's." Your attempt to pay the Lord for the gift would only show that you did not recognize the truth that you and all you have are already His. This is the terrible mistake which Simon Magus made when he offered to donate to the cause in payment for the gift of the Spirit. "But Peter said unto him, Thy money perish with thee, because thou hast thought that the *gift* of God may be purchased with money. Thou hast neither part nor lot in this matter; for thy heart is not right in the sight of God" (Acts 8:20, 21).

That one pleases the Lord who esteems the gift of the Holy Ghost so highly that he never thinks of purchasing it with prayers or good works, but who simply *receives* the *gift*, and thanks the Lord for it.

"For God so loved the world, that he gave his only begotten Son, that whosoever believeth in him should not perish, but have everlasting life" (John 3:16). "He that spared not his own Son, but delivered him up for us all, how shall he not *with him also freely give us all things?*" The gift of the Spirit is one of the *all things* which God gave us when He gave His Son. And this gift has been on deposit for us all the time, awaiting our demand and reception. Why not with Him freely receive "all things," which include the "gift of the Holy Ghost. For the promise is unto you, and to your children, and to all that are afar off, even as many as the Lord our God shall call" (Acts 2: 38, 39).

CHAPTER TWENTY-SIX

PRAYING FOR THE SPIRIT

It is not enough to recognize that there "be an Holy Ghost," it is not enough to recognize our need of the Spirit, neither is it enough to recognize that the Spirit is our birthright, nor the Lord's great willingness to give us His Spirit. Not one nor all of these will bring the baptism. The Lord wants us to recognize all this, and then He wants us to ask Him for the promised power. It is an old saying, and true as old, that anything that is worth having is worth asking for, and especially is it true in this connection.

He who is not sufficiently acquainted with the promise of the Spirit to desire it, is not qualified to become a channel for the gift, because he would not recognize the nature nor source of the power. And he whose knowledge of the nature and source of this great gift does not lead him to ask for the gift, would not appreciate it if he did receive it. And our perseverance in prayer for this gift will be measured by our appreciation of it.

But while it is clear from the nature of the case, that we should pray definitely for the promised Spirit,

139

yet we are plainly exhorted by the Word of God to
ask for the Holy Ghost, and to ask with importunity—
with pressing urgency.

In Luke 11:5–13 our Saviour presents the following
parable, with its application, to impress the need of earnest prayer for the Holy Spirit. That the parable is
given for this purpose is plain from the last sentence of
the Lord's application of the parable, as follows: "And
he said unto them, Which of you shall have a friend,
and shall go unto him at midnight, and say unto him,
Friend, lend me three loaves; for a friend of mine in his
journey is come to me, and I have nothing to set before
him? And he from within shall answer and say, Trouble me not; the door is now shut, and my children are
with me in bed; I can not rise and give thee. I say unto
you, Though he will not rise and give him, because he
is his friend, yet because of his importunity he will rise
and give him as many as he needeth. And I say unto
you, Ask, and it shall be given you; seek, and ye shall
find; knock, and it shall be opened unto you. For every
one that asketh receiveth; and he that seeketh findeth;
and to him that knocketh it shall be opened. If a son
shall ask bread of any of you that is a father, will he
give him a stone? or if he ask a fish, will he for a fish
give him a serpent? or if he shall ask an egg, will he
offer him a scorpion? If ye then, being evil, know how
to give good gifts unto your children; how much more
shall your heavenly Father give the Holy Spirit to
them that ask him?"

Reader, are you anxious to feed your friends spiritual food? Do you feel your poverty keenly? Does your
lack of bread pain you in the presence of hungry souls?

Do you long for bread to feed the famishing? Just in proportion as you long to feed the hungry, just in that proportion will you plead for power from on high; just in that proportion will you importune in prayer for the Holy Spirit until you receive as many loaves as you need. Then ask Him. Ask Him with importunity.

"If ye then, being evil, know how to give good gifts unto your children; how much more shall your heavenly Father give the Holy Spirit to them that *ask him.*"

CHAPTER TWENTY-SEVEN

THE LAYING ON OF HANDS

The laying on of hands in connection with the receiving of the Holy Spirit, is plainly taught in the Scriptures. Paul presents it as a part of the teaching of the gospel—a teaching which follows the teaching of baptism. It is presented as one of the "first principles."

"Wherefore let us cease to speak of the first principles of Christ, and press on unto perfection; not laying again a foundation of repentance from dead works, and of faith toward God, of the teaching of baptisms, and of *laying on of hands*, and of resurrection of the dead, and of eternal judgment" (Heb. 6:1, 2, R.V.).

The laying on of hands in Paul's teaching occupies the same place as the receiving of the Holy Spirit in Peter's teaching. Both follow baptism.

"Then Peter said unto them, Repent, and be baptized every one of you in the name of Jesus Christ for the remission of sins, and ye shall receive the gift of the Holy Ghost" (Acts 2:38).

144

The practice of the apostles is in harmony with this teaching.

"But when they [the Samaritans] believed Philip preaching the things concerning the kingdom of God, and the name of Jesus Christ, they were baptized, both men and women."

"Now when the apostles which were at Jerusalem heard that Samaria had received the Word of God, they sent unto them Peter and John; who, when they were come down, prayed for them, that they might receive the Holy Ghost (for as yet he was fallen on none of them; only they were baptized in the name of the Lord Jesus). Then laid they their hands on them, and they received the Holy Ghost" (Acts 8:12–17).

It seems strange that it is not apparent to all that the Lord has ordained that the Holy Ghost shall be received through the laying on of hands. Even Simon the sorcerer saw that.

"And when Simon saw that through laying on of the apostles' hands the Holy Ghost was given, he offered them money, saying, Give me also this power, that on whomsoever I lay hands, he shall receive the Holy Ghost" (Acts 8:18, 19).

"And it came to pass, that, while Apollos was at Corinth, Paul having passed through the upper coasts came to Ephesus; and finding certain disciples, he said unto them, Have ye received the Holy Ghost since ye believed? And they said unto him, We have not so much as heard whether there be any Holy Ghost. And he said unto them, Unto what then were ye baptized?

And they said, Unto John's baptism. Then said Paul, John verily baptized with the baptism of repentance, saying unto the people, that they should believe on him which should come after him, that is, on Christ Jesus. When they heard this, they were baptized in the name of the Lord Jesus. And when Paul had laid his hands upon them, the Holy Ghost came on them; and they spake with tongues, and prophesied" (Acts 19:1–6).

While it is true that "through laying on of the apostles' hands the Holy Ghost was given," it is also true that without the laying on of hands the Holy Ghost was given. Though Christ was baptized in water by the hands of John, yet he received the baptism with the Spirit directly from God. The apostles were all baptized with the Spirit on the day of Pentecost without the laying on of human hands. Cornelius and his household were baptized with the Holy Ghost without the laying on of human hands. (Acts 10:44-48).

But these are all exceptional cases, and only show that God does give His Spirit independent of the laying on of human hands. They do not in any way militate against the general rule. Just as in this last case the Lord baptized with the Holy Ghost *before* water-baptism, though His general plan, as stated through Peter, was to baptize with the Spirit *after* water-baptism; just so the Lord did baptize with the Holy Spirit without the laying on of human hands, though the general practice was that through "laying on of the apostles' hands the Holy Ghost was given."

In the case of the Gentiles of the house of Cornelius, it is evident that the Lord baptized them with the Holy Ghost before baptism by water and without the laying on of hands, simply because there was no one who was prepared to do it. The astonishment manifested by those of the circumcision that God should baptize the Gentiles at all, was evidence that they would not have baptized them with water, or laid hands on them to receive the Holy Ghost. This is further proven by the fact that before Peter administered water-baptism, he anticipated and met all protests by asking, "Can any man forbid water, that these should not be baptized, which have received the Holy Ghost as well as we?"

While it is true that through laying on of the apostles' hands the Holy Ghost was given, and that this is God's plan, it is also true that this most solemn service is but a hollow mockery where there is but the form without the power. Unless he who would lay on hands has apostolic power and the candidate apostolic preparation, better trust God to baptize with His Spirit in His own time without human hands, as He certainly did and certainly will. John was prepared to baptize our Lord with water, but not with the Holy Ghost. Philip, the evangelist, was qualified to do "miracles and signs" and to baptize with water, but it was "through the laying on of the apostles' hands" that "the Holy Ghost was given."

God will and does hear the cry of those who are consecrated, and gives them His Spirit in these days of unbelief in high places, without the laying on of hands, just as in these days of unbelief in *healing* He hears the cries of the afflicted and heals without the laying on of hands, though the Lord declares of those that believe, "They shall lay hands on the sick, and they shall recover" (Mark 16:18).

CHAPTER TWENTY-EIGHT

"BELIEVE THAT YE RECEIVE"

It is not enough to submit to the cleansing blood; it is not enough to consecrate that which is cleansed to the Cleanser; it is not enough to call upon Him with importunity. All this may be done, and you may still fail to "receive the promise of the Spirit" because, as the next two words teach, the promise of the Spirit is received *"through faith"* (Gal. 3:14. See also John 7:38 and Eph. 1:13).

"Let him ask in *faith, nothing wavering.* For he that wavereth is like a wave of the sea driven with the wind and tossed. For let not that man think that he shall receive anything of the Lord" (James 1:6, 7). The Lord is not pleased with the man who prays, however long and earnestly, who does not believe. "Without faith it is impossible to please him; for he that cometh to God must believe that he is, and that he *is a rewarder* of them that diligently seek him" (Heb. 11:6). He who diligently seeks God for that which He has promised, and then refuses to believe His promise, charges God with unfaithfulness. "He that believeth not God hath made him a liar." Unbelief, therefore, is

148

but another name for the sin of calling God a liar. Is it any wonder, then, that the Word of the Lord declares that "without faith it is impossible to please him"?

Is not the admonition in this text now in place: "What things soever ye desire, when ye pray, *believe that ye receive them,* and ye shall have them"? What! believe that I have received the Holy Spirit before I receive Him? No, indeed! Only believe that you receive the blessing *before* the blessing is *realized* or felt by some physical demonstration. If you wait for seeing or feeling before you will believe, you are not walking by faith, but by sight. But "we walk by faith, not by sight" (II Cor. 5:7). Like the wicked Jews, you are demanding a sign before you will believe. Of them Christ said, "A wicked and adulterous generation seeketh after a sign." You better separate from that company immediately.

But does the Lord want me to believe that He has heard my prayer and granted the witnessing power, without any evidence on which to base that belief? No, indeed! You have the strongest possible foundation for your faith. "Whosoever heareth these sayings of mine, and *doeth them,* I will liken him unto a wise man which built his house upon a rock; and the rain descended, and the floods came, and the winds blew, and beat upon that house; and it fell not; for it was founded upon a rock" (Matt. 7:24, 25).

Now, reader, watch for something to *do* in the following sayings of Christ: "What things soever ye desire, when ye pray, *believe that ye receive them,* and ye shall have them." Will you *do* it? Will you *believe* that you receive the Holy Spirit? If you *do believe*, the Lord wants you to be confident. He does not want a particle of doubt to remain. Here is your confidence: "This is the confidence that we have in him, that, if we ask anything according to his will, he heareth us. And if we know that he hear us, whatsoever we ask, we know that we have the petitions that we desired of him" (I John 5:14, 15).

You notice that the *confidence* depends on asking "*according* to his will." Now let us see if it is His will to give you His Holy Spirit. He says: "If ye then, being evil, know how to give good gifts unto your children; *how much more* shall your heavenly Father *give the Holy Spirit* to them *that* ask him?"

It was during the terrible blizzard of February, 1899. The streets of Brooklyn were blocked with snow. The streetcars were unable to run. For days no attempt was made to clear any but the great business thoroughfares. I was living on a side street. The snow was waist deep in places on our street, and still it stormed. Our baby girl of eighteen months became ill with a burning fever. All night she called for water. She was weak and would not eat, but still was able to walk. The following evening she was lying in her mother's lap. Presently she looked up and said through her parched lips, "Mama, apple." My wife looked at me with a pained expression, and said, "Papa, there isn't an apple in the house."

The baby heard her and, sliding down from her mother's lap, toddled over to where I sat, and putting one little hand on each of my knees, looked up into my face through her tired blue eyes and said, "Papa, apple." She did not think of the impossibilities; she did not look at the storm or the snow. She looked only at papa, and prayed for an apple. A determination came over me, too deep for words, which only could be expressed in *works*. I immediately arose and, putting on my stormcoat, threw myself into the drifts against the storm. I sometimes waded, and sometimes wallowed, but I was wonderfully happy, happy in the thought of bringing back an apple to reward the faith in that upturned face. And by and by I succeeded, and with added joy hurried back to the baby. As I was working my way back, the Spirit brought to my remembrance the words, "If ye then, being evil, know how to give good gifts unto your children; *how much more shall your heavenly Father give the Holy Spirit to them that ask him?*"

Yes, there is no doubt of His willingness. That is settled. "And this is the confidence that we have in him, that if we ask anything *according to his will*, he heareth us; and if we know that he hear us [and we do know, for we know that we have asked according to his will], *we know* that *we have* the petitions that we desired of him."

Reader, what is your petition? Is it that you may receive the Holy Ghost, power for witnessing for your Lord, power to tell what you know of His power to save to the uttermost? The Lord says you have your petition. If anyone asks you how you know, tell them that you base your confidence on the promise of God. One has put this truth thus:

"Many do not exercise that faith which it is their privilege and duty to exercise, often waiting for that feeling which faith alone can bring. Feeling is not faith; the two are distinct. Faith is ours to exercise, but joyful feeling and the blessing are God's to give. The grace of God comes to the soul through the channel of living faith, and that faith it is in our power to exercise.

"True faith lays hold of, and claims, the promised blessing before it is realized and felt. We must send up our petitions in faith within the second veil, and let our faith take hold of the promised blessing and claim it as ours. We are then to believe that we receive the blessing, because our faith has hold of it, and according to the Word it is ours. 'What things soever ye desire, when ye pray, believe that ye receive them, and ye shall have them.' Here is faith, naked faith, to believe that we receive the blessing even before we realize it. When the promised blessing is realized and enjoyed, faith is swallowed up. But many suppose they have much faith when sharing largely of the Holy Spirit, and they cannot have faith unless they *feel* the power of the Spirit. Such confound faith with the blessing that comes through faith. The very time to exercise faith is when we feel destitute of the Spirit. When thick clouds of darkness seem to hover over the mind, then is the time to let living faith pierce the darkness and scatter the cloud. True faith rests on the promises contained in the Word of God, and those only who obey that Word can claim its glorious promises. 'If ye abide in me, and my words abide in you, ye shall ask what ye will, and it shall be done unto you' (John 15:7). 'Whatsoever we ask, we receive of him, because we keep his commandments, and do those things that are pleasing in his sight' (I John 3:22)."

CHAPTER TWENTY-NINE

FAITH ILLUSTRATED

In Scripture Abraham is called the "father" of the faithful. And the reason he bears this name is because he is a striking example of one who believed God would do a miracle, and acted on his belief, without any other evidence than the naked word of God. Abraham obeyed the Lord in a case where obedience would make it necessary for God to perform a miracle to save himself from becoming untruthful. God had promised to Abraham that through Isaac—"with his seed"— He would establish His covenant to make Abraham a father of many nations. He then called upon Abraham to offer this same son as a sacrifice. If Abraham obeyed, his obedience would make it necessary for God to raise Isaac from the dead in order to save himself from being untruthful.

"By faith, Abraham, when he was tried, offered up Isaac; and he that had received the promises offered up his only begotten son, of whom it was said, that in Isaac shall thy seed be called; accounting that God was able to raise him up, even from the dead; from whence also he received him in a figure" (Heb. 11:17-19).

It greatly pleased the Lord to have Abraham act out his faith in the word of God, and thereby make it necessary for God to work a miracle to prove His word true. Now, don't you think that the Lord would be pleased to have you exercise faith in the promise of God, or act out your faith, even though that act requires that God shall again work a miracle to make His promise true to you?

But is not this what you have already done? When you believed the promise of the Lord for cleansing from sin, your faith made it necessary for the Lord to perform a miracle to sustain His Word. Again, when you believed His promise to deliver you from that great temptation, your faith made it necessary for God to work another miracle to make His promise sure to you. Now, the Lord promises to baptize you with the Holy Spirit for witnessing, and He wants you to believe that promise.

He knows that your faith will make it necessary for Him to work a miracle to keep His word, but this is just what the Lord asks you to do, and this is just what will please Him. "Without faith [without believing God when a miracle is necessary to sustain His promise], it is impossible to please him."

To the man who was palsied, the Lord said, "Rise, take up thy bed, and walk." But that was just what the paralytic could not do. He might have said, "Master, if you will heal me, then I will arise; but I am paralyzed; I cannot rise and walk. I want to be healed so I can arise and walk." But then he would not be acting out his faith. And a faith that does not *act* is dead.

"Faith, if it have not works, is dead." "A man will say, Thou hast faith, and I have works; show me thy faith apart from thy works, and I *by my works will show thee my faith*" (James 2:17, 18, R.V.).

No faith appears in its perfection until it *acts*. But how could a paralytic act? If there was a muscle in his body that he could use in an attempt to rise, faith would lead him to use that muscle. And if every muscle were paralyzed, he could manifest his faith by willingness to arise. Though paralyzed, he was called upon by the Lord to act like a man who was not paralyzed; and it was the man's part to act like a well man, and the Lord's part to *see that he was well*.

Ten lepers came to Christ to be healed. He said, "Go show yourselves unto the priests." They might have answered: "Cleanse us, Lord, and then we will go. It is unlawful for us to appear before the priest in our leprosy; only those who are cleansed show themselves to the priest." But Christ had said, "Go."

Faith said: "The Master said, 'Go.' It is true that only cleansed men show themselves to the priest, and in going we have to act like cleansed men, when these loathsome bodies bear testimony that we are not cleansed. But let us go, and leave appearances and results with Him. Let us go." And they went. And *"as they went, they were cleansed"* (Luke 17:14).

Thus from both precept and practice it is plain that true faith claims the promise and acts upon it before that promise is realized and felt. This is the faith which our Lord taught and commended. It is the faith that pleases Him. Should we, then, fear to do that which pleases Him? It is not presumption to do what the Lord commands. It is presumption to refuse to do it.

You *believe* the promise of God to give you His Holy Spirit. You yield yourself wholly to the Lord, ask for the promise of the Spirit, accept it by faith. Just as sure as you do this God will fulfil His word to you. If you believe the promise, if you believe that you have received the promise of the Spirit, God supplies the fact; you have the power from on high as truly as the paralytic was healed when he believed he was healed. It *is* so if you believe it. Do not wait to *feel* you are filled with the Spirit, but say: "I believe it. It *is* so, not because I feel it, but because God has promised it." "What things soever ye desire, when ye pray, *believe that ye receive them, and ye shall have them.*"

More witnessing by letter:

"Praise the Lord, the anchor still holds! I thank Him for the victories I have gained. I praise His holy name for the power to keep me from sinning, and for the Holy Spirit for service. With His help, I will go through to the end."

*   *   *   *   *

"I am rejoicing in the conscious presence of the Holy Spirit, and at times the Spirit of the Lord comes mightily upon me. I find that the only hope for victory over self and sin is in the Holy Spirit's coming mightily upon me. I bless the Lord that in the crises of my soul, the Spirit of God comes in to set up a standard against the enemy."

*   *   *   *   *

"I have much to praise the Lord for this afternoon for the change He has wrought in my heart. I know He has given me His Holy Spirit who will keep me from falling. My Bible seems like a new book to me; I understand it better now, for it is being translated into my own life."

*   *   *   *   *

"You understand me when I say there is a new song in my life. The work of the Holy Spirit abides in our midst. With all the service of my life, I am sure I cannot show my gratitude for His last blessing so graciously bestowed upon us here. The richest of all blessings is the gift of the Holy Ghost. Oh, what a comfort! No heart can express it; no tongue nor life can express the joy that comes by the Spirit of Christ dwelling in our hearts. Brother ———— has a live testimony. He attends meetings at the mission (something new for him). He certainly rejoices in deliverance. It makes our hearts glad to see and hear him. On the part of many more in the church there is now a new interest for the mission work. The church is going forward. There is a company here who are going through in the strength of Jesus. The Lord is granting us victory over sins daily. It is all in believing and trusting. There is a blessed assurance. No possibility of defeat when trusting our Lord and Saviour."

CHAPTER THIRTY

PERSONAL EXPERIENCE IN RECEIVING

"Ye are my witnesses, saith the Lord."

The writer desires at this point to bear personal witness to the faithfulness of God in fulfilling His promise to give us His Spirit for witnessing in response to faith. I know that it behooves one to be modest in respect to this matter. But why should it be thought egotistical to confess our Lord's faithfulness in answering the cry of faith for power from on high, to give force to an otherwise spiritless witness, any more than to confess to His faithfulness to forgive our sins or keep us from falling?

I came to a point in my ministry where I hungered for power to impress the great truths of the gospel upon the hearts of the people. I saw sin flourishing on every hand like a green bay tree. I saw worldliness flooding the churches. I saw ministers resorting to this and that worldly method to interest the people. I saw many seeking for the regeneration of society through legislative enactments.

I became convinced that all these were but miserable substitutes for the "power from on high"; that instead of lobbying for human power in legislative halls, the Christian should tarry at the throne of grace until endued with power from on high. The conviction became overwhelming, so much so that I cried out in anguish of soul at the close of my sermon, "I must have power from on high."

This conviction deepened. I commenced to talk about it, and write about it—to *exhort others* to receive it. I had finished an article for publication, on this subject, with the words, "Not by might, nor by power, but by my Spirit, saith the Lord of hosts." I was sitting with my eyes riveted on these words when the Spirit of the Lord suggested to my mind the searching question: "Is that Scripture a part of *your* experience? Do *you* know its meaning? Are you not, like a parrot, repeating it to others while not knowing its meaning yourself?"

With tears I confessed that all this was true, but then and there I asked the Lord definitely to make the Scripture a part of my experience. This was in the afternoon. The night following I lay awake thinking of the prayer that I had offered, and still longing for its fulfilment, when suddenly this Scripture fastened itself on my mind, "What things soever ye desire, when ye pray, believe that ye receive them, and ye shall have them." I had found that Scripture true in seeking forgiveness of sins and keeping power, but had not thought of it in this connection. In my surprise and simplicity, I said to the Lord, "Is it as easy as that?" and immediately that other blessed Scripture flashed on my mind,

"If ye then, being evil, know how to give good gifts unto your children; *how much more* shall your heavenly Father give the Holy Spirit to them that ask him?" And I believed Him, and then and there thanked Him for the Holy Spirit.

Reader, did I do right? You answer, "Yes." Then, go and do thou likewise.

But some trembling soul will venture to ask, "How did you feel? I didn't feel any different. "Well, how did you know that it was so?" Because the Word of the Lord said it was so. What did I need of a manifestation of witnessing power then, when I was all alone, with no one to whom I could bear witness? I had prayed the Lord for the Holy Ghost to give power to my testimony when I witnessed for Him. Why should the Lord turn on the power then and rattle the empty machine before there was grain to be threshed out? I had asked for the Holy Ghost for service; and when an opportunity to serve came, the power would be present.

So I believed, and so it was and ever has been. Praise the Lord! "Have you ever experienced any feeling?" someone will ask. Oh, yes, all that was good for me—all I could stand; but it came as the *result* of my faith, not my faith as the result of my feeling. "What things soever ye desire, when ye pray, believe that ye receive them, and ye shall have them."

CHAPTER THIRTY-ONE

PERSONAL EXPERIENCE IN WITNESSING

"We are his witnesses of these things; and so is also the Holy Ghost, whom God hath given to them that obey him" (Acts 5:32).

At the closing service of a series of revival meetings, a man past middle age arose and said:

"I am an agnostic, but I am having more difficulty accounting for the manifestation of power which I have witnessed during these meetings than with all the difficult questions regarding the inspiration of the Scriptures. Pray for me that I may find the truth."

Prayer was offered for him, and according to the opinion of his wife, which is generally good testimony, he was converted.

What was it that softened and subdued the heart of this unbeliever? It was none other than the power of that other Witness, the Holy Spirit, which had borne witness with the witness of the servants of God of what they had seen and heard.

"There are some who have come from a neighboring city and who cannot remain for the evening meeting," said the messenger. "They have sent me to request a service at five o'clock."

I was tired with the incessant labor of the meeting, but the thought that there were people hungry enough for the gospel to make request for an added service was refreshing.

The Lord indicated the theme, while a brother minister opened the meeting with prayer, and then followed thirty minutes of witnessing to the power of the gospel to save.

After the benediction, a brother hurried to the desk and, with face beaming with joy, said: "The arrow of truth has done its work. Mr. ———, the neighborhood infidel, is deep under conviction, and sits yonder with his head resting on the chair in front of him, weeping. Come and speak with him." Substantially the following conversation was the result of the interview:

Infidel: I am getting old, as you see by these gray hairs, and yet I am without an anchor. I am helplessly drifting. I tried to anchor in infidelity and failed. Then I tried to find an anchor in Spiritualism, but it does not satisfy me.

Minister: What you need is the Saviour; receive Him, and you will have an anchor.

Infidel: How?

Minister: Confess your sins and ask the Lord to forgive as He promises to do. Believe that He forgives and receives you. "Him that cometh to me I will in no wise cast out," is the promise.

Infidel: I cannot believe. I have been accustomed to explain away all the phenomena of what you call faith, on psychological grounds, and I cannot believe.

Minister: I can. Once I was a helpless, hopeless, wreck; but the Lord has wrought a miracle in my life, and is giving me the victory over these things which once enslaved me. I know He can save you because He is saving me.

Infidel: That is what impressed me. I see you have something in your life that I don't have. You are anchored, while I am drifting.

Minister: Now, my brother, you acknowledge that you are in need of salvation, and you believe that I have the salvation you want. Hadn't you better accept it, too? If you should consult a trusted physician, and he should accurately describe your affliction and then prescribe a treatment which had resulted in his cure, would you not be acting wisely to faithfully follow it?

Infidel: Yes.

Minister: Will you not take the treatment which I prescribe, and which has healed me?

Infidel: I will try.

Then we found a retired spot, and kneeling he acknowledged his transgressions and pleaded for pardon. Kneeling by his side, I watched the struggle with intense interest, answering each despairing cry of doubt with a promise of the Word. Presently he prayed: "I will act on the promise; I accept forgiveness. I am forgiven. But, Lord, what did you forgive me for? Will I fall back again into my old sins? Will I get angry again? Will I again be profane as I have been? I am afraid I will bring disgrace on Christianity. O Lord, I am afraid!"

At this crisis I placed my Bible, open at Isa. 41:10, before his face, which he read aloud slowly:

"Fear thou not; for I am with thee; be not dismayed; for I am thy God; I will strengthen thee; yea, I will help thee; yea, I will uphold thee with the right hand of my righteousness."

This Scripture completed the victory, and we returned triumphant to find many of his Christian neighbors anxiously waiting the outcome of the struggle. Ministers and people, without regard to denomination, gathered around him to rejoice with him over his new-found hope. After thanking the Lord for the victory, I sat alone, meditating over the meeting and its results.

"What did I say that moved him?" I queried. "All I did was to witness to the power of God to save. The witness was neither deep nor eloquent. It was but the simple story, simply told."

It was none other than the Holy Spirit that had done the work. He had taken the witness I bore, and given it power to convince and convict.

"Ye shall receive power, after that the Holy Ghost is come upon you; and ye shall be witnesses unto me."

"What is this?" said a burly man, gruffly, to a companion, as we sat in front of a mission in a southern city.

"It is a mission," replied the brother meekly.

"What is a mission?" was the next question, which quickly followed with caustic contempt in the tone.

"It is where they preach——"

"Preach what?" broke in the man.

"Preach the gospel," was the response.

"What is the gospel?"

The brother hesitated a moment at this point under the man's rough, rapid questioning. This was my opportunity, and with firm confidence and a faith based on the knowledge of the presence of the heavenly Witness, I said:

"The gospel is the power of God to save a man from doing those things which he would like to stop doing and can't." At this he turned and looked at me with an awakened interest. Looking him straight in the eyes, I repeated the definition with a personal witness to its truthfulness.

"Partner, that's what I need. I am a good workman, and have no trouble finding a job. I have just struck the town. I've money; I don't want your money. I shall soon get a job; but when I have worked a couple of weeks and received my wages, then I shall get drunk and lose my job, and I shall have to move on to another city. I have been doing this for twenty-five years." At this his voice trembled, and his giant form shook with emotion.

"You can be saved from all that," I said with increasing confidence. "And the reason I know is because the Lord has saved me from a slavery as bad as yours. I believe the Lord never undertook a harder case than when He undertook to save me; and I know He can save you."

"Tell me how," said the man as he took my hand between the calloused palms of his giant hands and, all subdued and gentle as a lamb, listened while I told him the way of salvation. And when it was told, he departed with a new-born hope.

What transformed the lion into a lamb? What was it that changed this burly, brutish man into a tearful, trembling, teachable child? It was that other Witness that had taken the witness of a mortal man, and with His own promised power, driven it through the calloused heart of this home-born heathen. Praise the Lord for the power from on high!

"May I have a talk with you, Brother Ballenger?" asked a nine-year-old girl at the close of the meeting. A time was set, and the youthful seeker came and told her troubles, and asked that prayer might be offered for her. There was great earnestness in her conversation, and tears and sobs broke into her intelligent prayer.

From others it was learned that her adoptive mother, who had taken her when two years old, had thought it absolutely necessary to separate this child from her family because she dreaded the results of certain sinful habits upon the younger adopted children. This decision brought great suffering to both adoptive parents, for they loved the child.

The situation, summed up, was this: A nine-year-old child confessing her sins and weeping before God in prayer for deliverance from sinning; a loving mother weeping and praying for her deliverance; and the life of the Lord Jesus Christ given for her salvation and pleading in her behalf at the Father's throne. And yet the child continues to sin, and so seriously that she is deemed dangerous and is sent forth from the home as incorrigible.

No encouraging results followed our prayer season. The help must come through the cooperation of the adoptive mother, for her own salvation.

Months later I met the adoptive mother and heard from her the sad story again. Her heart yearned for the child, but she feared to let the little outcast come home. The little sinner wanted to go home and be good; the mother wanted her to come home and be good; the Lord wanted her to come home and be good; yet she was bad, and was banished from home.

When these facts were laid before the mother in this light, it was decided that the devil was not strong enough to keep the little one from home and deliverance, in opposition to the desire of the child, her mother, and her God. We, therefore, knelt and presented the child at the throne of grace with holy boldness. We told the Lord that we did not believe the enemy had power enough to ruin the child in the face of such a combination of cries for deliverance. We claimed deliverance by faith. The mother arose from her knees with faith to call the little wanderer home. The result of her faith is here told in her own words:

"For some time I have been impressed to write to you to the glory of God, but have felt that it would be wrong unnecessarily to take a moment of your time, which otherwise would be spent to the glory of God. But my heart is so full this morning that I cannot forbear writing. Doubtless you will not remember me unless I refer to the case of the little girl, ———, whom you talked with at ———, and who seemed such an extraordinary case. I am ———, who was helped spiritually and physically through your efforts at the ——— camp meeting. My heart is full of praise and gratitude for the goodness of the Lord to me. I claimed the victory over sin in all its phases at that time, and claim it still. Be untiring in your efforts to inspire others with the same faith that you preached at our camp meeting. I had been groping for help. It was dark, but I held on, and my prayer was more than answered at the camp meeting. My faith has grown a hundredfold. Since then *I live* by faith. Many and varied have been my experiences, but they have all been permitted for my good, as they have tended to strengthen my faith. And the Lord has permitted my experiences to be a help to others, for which I praise Him.

"I asked for your prayers in behalf of little ———, and I have felt that I had them. I have taken her back into my heart and home. I have claimed the keeping

power with and for her, and I thank God that now I
see a change for the better. We seek the Lord earnestly
and untiringly; and the very fact that she, over whom
Satan seemed to have almost entire control, is being
moulded into the likeness of Christ, demonstrates the
power of God and the truthfulness of the Scripture
which says, 'What things soever ye desire, when ye
pray, believe that ye receive them, and ye shall have
them.' Oh, I am so glad I have learned to trust in
Jesus! He gives me strength to do more than I have
been able to do in thirteen years. I live by faith, and
I praise the dear Lord for the privilege of so doing."

More extracts from letters received:

"When you were here, I thought that if I could only
be with you all the time, in meetings, we could feel the
Spirit's power continually, though you said we would
not miss you. I have not missed you, as the Comforter
has made His abode with us. Praise the Lord! Yes,
'the anchor holds.' "

* * * * *

"I can say with more assurance than ever that the
time you spent in the ———church was a refreshing
shower of the Spirit of God. *It continues*, praise the
Lord! Among the good testimonies of the brethren
and sisters, we hear many of the expressions you used
to strengthen our faith. To the testimony you bore, we
can daily say, 'Amen.' The same good Spirit that
wrought in your heart to bring you to this blessed experience in Christ, is now manifest in our church. . . .
Others are coming and finding a home where Jesus
has prepared a place for himself to dwell. Who would
not dwell in this home? I praise the Lord I can say
without a doubt, 'We are onward; no falling back.' "

CHAPTER THIRTY-TWO

THE FRUIT BEFORE THE GIFTS

Reader, are you seeking the fulness of the Holy Spirit for service in the work of the Lord? If so, you are seeking for the *gifts* of the Spirit. For everyone who is baptized with the Spirit for *service* in the cause of Christ is thereby given one or more of the *gifts* of the Spirit. But before you can have *one* of the gifts of the Spirit in its fulness, you must have *every one* of the manifestations of the *fruit* of the Spirit. It is the plan of God to *divide* the *gifts* of the Spirit, "dividing to every man severally as he will"; but He *never divides* the *fruit*. The fruit of the Spirit cannot be separated and divided among the members of the church, giving to one "love" and to another "longsuffering." One cannot say, "I have love, and you have longsuffering and kindness" (R.V.), for he that has love has longsuffering and kindness, and he that has longsuffering and kindness has love, because love, and love only, is longsuffering and kind; "love suffereth long, and is kind" (I Cor. 13:4, R.V.). Neither can one say, "I have love and you have meekness," for love is meek; "love is not puffed up" (verse 4).

He that offendeth in one point of the royal law is guilty of all (James 2:10). So he who *lacks one* of the manifestations of the fruit of the Spirit *lacks every one.* It is impossible for one to possess the "love" and "joy" of the Spirit, and in the place of the "peace" of the Spirit manifest "strife," the fruit of the flesh. Neither can one possess the kindness and meekness of the Spirit and manifest emulation, hatred, and wrath, which are works of the flesh. As well claim to have the Son without the Father, or the Holy Ghost without the Father and Son, as to claim to have one manifestation of the fruit of the Spirit and not the others.

Reader, you either possess *every one* of the manifestations of the fruit of the Spirit, or you possess *none.* This is a terribly solemn truth, but there is no denying it. Now read the description of the fruit of the Spirit slowly, and meditate seriously, and see if it is the fruit your life is bearing.

"The fruit of the Spirit is love, joy, peace, long-suffering, kindness, goodness, faithfulness, meekness, temperance; against such there is no law" (Gal. 5:22, 23, R.V.).

Do not despair if the torch of truth discovers only leaves. The first step toward fruit-bearing is the discovery of lack of fruit. Have you discovered a lack? Do you want to bear the fruit of the Spirit? The Lord wants you to bear the fruit of the Spirit, and He knows you cannot bear this fruit alone. Hear Him speak:

"As the branch cannot bear fruit of itself, except it abide in the vine; no more can ye, except ye abide in me. I am the vine, ye are the branches. He that abideth in me, and I in him, the same bringeth forth much fruit; for without me ye can do nothing."

"Herein is my Father glorified, that ye bear much fruit; so shall ye be my disciples. As the Father hath loved me, so have I loved you; continue ye in my love. If ye keep my commandments, ye shall abide in my love; even as I have kept my Father's commandments, and abide in his love" (John 15:4, 5, 8–10).

Why does the Lord speak these tender words to *you?* Hear Him again: "These things have I spoken unto you, that my joy might remain in you, and that your joy might be full" (John 15:11). The Lord wants you to bear much fruit both for His joy and your joy. But the Lord knows you cannot bear the fruit of the Spirit without the indwelling Spirit. Therefore, it will bring joy to the Lord to give you the fruit-bearing Spirit.

"But," you say, "how shall I *receive* that which it is His joy to give?" Give Him your whole body as a perpetual temple for the Holy Spirit. "Neither yield ye your members as instruments of unrighteousness unto sin; but yield yourselves unto God, as those that are alive from the dead, and your members as instruments of righteousness unto God. For sin shall not have dominion over you" (Rom. 6:13, 14).

Will you do this? Will you do it *now?* Have you done it? Is it now done? Do you now yield every fiber of your being, every faculty of your mind, every organ of your body, every plan of your life, every earthly possession, your occupation, home, family, and friends, to the Lord, to be His *now* and *forever?*

Now you have reached the crisis. Here is where the rich young man failed. Here is where the proud young woman fails. If you refuse to make this entire surrender, it will be useless for you to read further.

Having surrendered yourself to the Lord for the bearing of the fruit of the Spirit, throw open the door of your heart and ask the Lord to come in by His Spirit. He says, "Behold, I stand at the door, and knock; if any man hear my voice, and open the door, I will come in to him, and will sup with him, and he with me" (Rev. 3:20). Open the door and ask Him in. "Ask, and it shall be given you. . . . Every one that asketh receiveth. . . . If ye then, being evil, know how to give good gifts unto your children; how much more shall your heavenly Father give the Holy Spirit to them that ask him?" (Luke 11:9–13).

Someone will say, "Now that I have asked Him for the Spirit that I may bear fruit, what shall I do next?" Let the Lord answer: "What things soever ye desire, when ye pray, believe that ye receive them, and ye shall have them" (Mark 11:24). Now do not wait to *feel* that you have the Spirit, but say, "I have the Spirit; not because I feel that I have Him, but because God has promised to give the Spirit to me if I ask, and I have asked, and to doubt would be to charge God with unfaithfulness. 'He that believeth not God hath made him a liar.' "

Do you not think that the Lord would be pleased if you believe His promise? Then believe that you receive His Spirit, and please Him. Do it *now*.

The reasons why the fruit of the Spirit must appear in all its manifestations before one manifestation of the gifts of the Spirit can appear, will be presented in the next chapter.

CHAPTER THIRTY-THREE

HOW TO SEEK SPIRITUAL GIFTS

The *fruit* of the Spirit must appear in the life of the Christian; the *gifts* of the Spirit may not. Millions will be saved who never had the gift of miracles, but not one will ever be saved who did not possess the fruit of love. Many will be saved who never spake with tongues, but none will be saved who did not have the fruit of temperance.

The fruit of the Spirit is eternal. "Love never faileth." The gifts of the Spirit are only temporal. "Whether there be prophecies, they shall be done away; whether there be tongues, they shall cease" (I Cor. 13:8, R.V.). The fruit of the Spirit is the material which composes the house eternal. The gifts are but the temporary staging used for the building of the house, "for the perfecting of the saints, unto the work of ministering, unto the building up of the body of Christ" (Eph. 4:12, R.V.).

"But when that which is perfect is come, then that which is in part shall be done away" (I Cor. 13:10).

When the building is perfected, the staging is taken away; so when the body of Christ is perfected, the gifts will be taken away.

What would a man with the gift of prophecy do with this gift in heaven? What need would he have of visions of the glories of heaven when face to face with its glories? What would the discerner of spirits do with his gift in heaven where there is but one Spirit? Of what use would be the gift of tongues, or the interpretation of tongues in heaven, where all speak one language? What would the evangelist do with his gift where all are eternally saved? Therefore as the tools of a building are to a building, so are the gifts of the Spirit to the fruit of the Spirit. A builder who did not understand and appreciate the relation of the tools and staging to the edifice, would not be a competent builder, and could not be trusted with either tools or building. So he who does not understand and appreciate the relation of the gifts of the Spirit to the fruit of the Spirit, cannot and will not be entrusted by the great Master-builder with the gifts of the Spirit for the work of building up the body of Christ.

He who seeks to manifest the gifts of the Spirit before he manifests the fruit of the Spirit, thereby shows that he is not in a condition to be trusted with the gifts. He who seeks miracles before meekness will never be entrusted with the gift of working miracles. He who follows after the gift of tongues more earnestly than after the grace of temperance is not fitted to use even the one tongue he already has. He who covets the gift of healing more earnestly than the grace of love, is himself in need of healing before he can be entrusted with the gift of healing.

Here is the story of two men who wanted the gift of working miracles, when they were not in possession of the grace of longsuffering.

The Lord was on His way to Jerusalem to attend the Passover feast. He was preaching in the towns through which He passed. James and John were sent to "a village of the Samaritans, to make ready for him." But the Samaritans "did not receive him, because his face was as though he would go to Jerusalem," and they were bitterly opposed to going to attend the feast at Jerusalem and to anyone who would go. This displeased James and John. They did not have that love that "suffereth long." They ought to have sought it. But instead, they sought the gift of working miracles. If they had possessed the gift, they would have quickly exercised it, burned up the Samaritans, and reported the destruction to the Lord. But they did not have the gift, and must go to Christ to obtain it. But instead of receiving it, they received a stinging rebuke: "Ye know not what manner of spirit ye are of. For the Son of man is not come to destroy men's lives, but to save them."

Any man possessed of power but destitute of love is a dangerous man. Power without love has made all the tyrants that ever reigned. Power without love is what makes the devil what he is.

So important is the subject of spiritual gifts that Paul devotes three chapters of his first letter to the

Corinthian church to its consideration; but not one word is spoken to discourage the Corinthians in their zeal after spiritual gifts. On the other hand, speaking by the Holy Ghost, he three times exhorts them to "desire earnestly" spiritual gifts. It is the ignorance concerning, not the zeal for, spiritual gifts that the Holy Spirit rebukes. After proving that all the gifts are needed, the apostle commands them to "desire earnestly the greater gifts" (I Cor. 12:31, R.V.). It was not their zeal in seeking spiritual gifts which was rebuked. In their ignorance and carnality they had sought the gifts through pride, strife, jealousy, and envy. (I Cor. 3:3). But Paul through the Spirit points out a "more excellent way" to seek them; and this way is shown in the thirteenth chapter and in the first verse of the fourteenth to be to seek first the fruit of the Spirit and afterwards the gifts of the Spirit.

After showing the immortality and importance of love, how that without this fruit of the Spirit, all the gifts of the Spirit are "sounding brass" and "nothing" (verses 1 to 3, R.V.), Paul, not wishing to quench their zeal for spiritual gifts, sums up the whole matter in this command, *"Follow after love; yet desire earnestly spiritual gifts"* (I Cor. 14:1, R.V.).

This is the "more excellent way" to seek for spiritual gifts. They must be sought through the love of the Spirit, through the love of Christ, that love which led Him to give up all for the salvation of sinning men. He who has that love will be led by it to desire earnestly to share in the gifts of the Spirit. Just in proportion as the builder loves the work of building, just in that same proportion will he seek the necessary tools and staging. So with the workers together with Christ; just in proportion as they love to build up the body of Christ, not themselves, just in that same proportion will they seek the gifts of the Spirit.

Do you long to see the unbelieving saved as a result of the exercise of the gifts? The Spirit declares that the unbeliever "will fall down on his face and worship God, declaring that God is among you indeed" (I Cor. 14:25, R.V.). Do the builders need that power today? Then, reader, let us seek it. Let us obey the commands of the Spirit, and seek the gifts of the Spirit, but seek them in the more excellent way marked out. *"Follow after love; yet desire earnestly spiritual gifts."* Reader, this is a command of God. Will you obey it?

CHAPTER THIRTY-FOUR

MIRACLES OF HEALING

"*Why* should it be thought a thing incredible with you, that God should raise the dead?" was the pointed, pleading question which Paul, the apostle, addressed to Agrippa, the king. Agrippa believed the prophets. Why should you believe the prophets, and discredit the resurrection? was the real import of Paul's searching question.

This question was followed by Paul's testimony concerning the miracle of his own conversion, and then the miracle of the resurrection of Christ in fulfilment of the promise of the prophets.

Why should it be thought a thing incredible with you that God should heal the sick? is another pointed question that pleads today for answer from those who profess to accept the testimony of Scripture.

The gospel of salvation is nothing if not a miracle. It is the "mystery of God," the working of a miraculous power, the effects of which can be seen and heard, but its processes are unexplained (John 3:8). It is easy for one who has experienced the miraculous transforma-

185

tion of life, called in Scripture the new birth, to credit the miracle of the resurrection of the body. And he who really believes in the resurrection of the body can readily believe in the healing of the body, which is only a kind of firstfruits, or part payment, of the promised "redemption of our body."

The atonement embraces the whole man, spirit, soul, and body. "I pray God your whole spirit and soul and body be preserved blameless unto the coming of our Lord Jesus Christ" (I Thess. 5:23). Notice how the promises of bodily healing are united with those of soul-healing in the following Scriptures:

"Bless the Lord, O my soul, ... who forgiveth all thine iniquities; who healeth all thy diseases" (Ps. 103:2, 3).

"He cast out the spirits with his word, and healed all that were sick; that it might be fulfilled which was spoken by Esaias the prophet, saying, Himself took our infirmities, and bare our sicknesses" (Matt. 8:16, 17).

Let us place this Scripture concerning our infirmities and sicknesses alongside another concerning our sins:

"Who his own self bare our sins in his own body on the tree" (I Peter 2:24).

"Himself took our infirmities, and bare our sicknesses" (Matt. 8:17).

Why did He bear our sins? *Answer*: "That we, being dead to sins, should live unto righteousness" (I Peter 2:24). "How shall we, that are dead to sin, live any longer therein?" (Rom. 6:2). "He hath made him to be sin for us, who knew no sin; that we might be made the righteousness of God in him" (II Cor. 5:21). "Thou shalt call his name Jesus; for he shall save his people *from their sins*" (Matt. 1:21). "He was manifested to *take away our sins.*"

Thus do the Scriptures teach that *He* bore our sins that *we* might not bear them. He bore them for us that He might bear them away from us; that we should bear them no longer. This is the blessed truth which we teach the sinner when he comes to us seeking salvation from sin.

Why did He take our infirmities and bear our sicknesses? Let the Scriptures answer, while we watch for the *taking away* of the *"infirmities"* and *"sicknesses"* from the infirm and sick.

"And, behold, there was a woman which had a spirit of infirmity eighteen years, and was bowed together, and could in no wise lift up herself. And when Jesus saw her, he called her to him, and said unto her, Woman, thou art *loosed from thine infirmity.* And he laid hands on her; and immediately she was *made straight,* and glorified God" (Luke 13:11–13).

"Then they went out to see what was done; and came to Jesus, and found the man, out of whom the devils *were departed,* sitting at the feet of Jesus, clothed, and in his right mind" (Luke 8:35).

"And as soon as he had spoken, immediately the *leprosy departed* from him, and he was cleansed" (Mark 1:42).

"And a certain man was there, which had an *infirmity* thirty and eight years. . . . Jesus saith unto him, Rise, take up thy bed, and walk. And immediately the man was *made whole*, and took up his bed, and walked" (John 5:5, 8, 9). "Great multitudes came together to hear, and to be healed by him of their *infirmities*" (Luke 5:15). "And Jesus went about all the cities and villages, teaching in their synagogues, and preaching the gospel of the kingdom, and *healing every sickness* and every disease among the people" (Matt. 9:35).

"And he touched her hand, and the *fever left her;* and she arose, and ministered unto them. When the even was come, they brought unto him many that were possessed with devils; and he cast out the spirits with his word, and healed all that were sick; that it might be fulfilled which was spoken by Esaias the prophet, saying, Himself took our infirmities, and bare our sicknesses" (Matt. 8:14–17).

From all these Scriptures it is clear that our Lord took all our infirmities and bare our sicknesses that we might not have to bear them; that we might be loosed from them; that they might depart from us. Jesus bore them, therefore, that He might bear them away from us that we might bear them no more.

All this proves that the gospel includes salvation from sickness as well as salvation from sin. At this point we shall be tempted to measure this truth by our limited experience. We are in danger of denying the inevitable conclusion to which the Scriptures have brought us, because we have never seen such mighty miracles of healing as are promised in the gospel, and which appear in the preaching and practice of that gospel at the hands of the apostolic church. But instead of cutting and trimming this tremendous truth to fit our experience, let us accept it in its fulness, however impossible it may seem to us, and commence immediately to enlarge our faith and experience until they shall measure up to apostolic precept and practice.

But why should anyone who believes in the miracle of conversion ever question the miracle of healing? "Whether is it easier to say to the sick of the palsy, Thy sins be forgiven thee; or to say, Arise, and take up thy bed, and walk?" (Mark 2:9). Reader, answer this question which the Lord asks *you*. Do not answer it from the standpoint of your limited experience, but from the interpretation of these promises as they appear in the practice of the apostolic church.

Why is it that a reported healing creates so much amazement among the people? If the Lord should today give sight to one born blind, it would cause a sensation throughout all Christendom. We would expect the world to wonder, but why should the church stand in amazement? If conversion is in reality a miracle, it is the greatest of all miracles. Why should there not be as much amazement manifested in the presence of this miracle? Does not the surprise manifested over miracles of healing show a lack of appreciation of the miracle of the new birth, and a disposition to transfer it from the realm of the miraculous to the sphere of the natural?

No one will ever be able to appreciate the miracle which follows the command, "Arise, and take up thy bed, and walk," until that one appreciates the miracle which follows the words, "Son, thy sins be forgiven thee."

In this I am not penning theory, but personal experience. The time was when I had no real faith in miracles of healing. I had not experienced God's miraculous saving and keeping power. But when this miracle appeared in my life, immediately there followed faith in God's power to heal the sick. I reasoned thus: God has wrought a mighty miracle in my life in delivering me from my besetting sins which have enslaved me all my life. It will require no greater miracle to heal the sick than He is manifesting in my life in keeping me from falling into my old sins. Thus arose my faith in God's healing power for the body. And as I received it, so must I walk in it. If there comes a shadow of a failure in my personal experience touching my salvation from sinning, there is a corresponding failure in my faith and practice concerning the healing of the sick.

There are conditions, of course, which must be met in order to realize salvation both from sin and sickness, which will be presented later; but we must not await the conditions before accepting the scriptural truth that the gospel includes health for the body as well as for the soul. To those who believe the Scriptures, I repeat the question, "Why should it be thought a thing incredible with you that God should heal the sick?"

CHAPTER THIRTY-FIVE

THE GIFTS OF THE SPIRIT WITHHELD

It had been a long time since the manifestation of miracles. Israel was sorely pressed by the Midianites. The wonderful miracles of the Exodus were only about two hundred years old, but those who witnessed them were dead. It looked to the sinning Israel as if miracles were at an end. Some doubtless were ready to deny that there ever had been miracles. At this time an angel appeared to Gideon, and informed him that a miracle was about to be wrought for the deliverance of his people. Gideon himself was tempted to think miracles were confined to the fathers, and he answered, "Where be all his miracles which our fathers told us of?" (Judges 6:13). After the miracles of the fire and of the fleece, he believed.

Gideon collected an army of 32,000 men, but when tested, 22,000 of them were found to entertain the conviction that the days of miracles were past, and were allowed to follow their convictions home. For good reasons, 9,700 of the remaining 10,000 were sent home. The remaining 300 believed that God would perform a miracle in their day, and He did.

Many today are perplexed, as was Gideon, over the absence of miracles in the church. They do not believe that miracles ended with the lives of the apostles, much less do they attempt to explain away the scriptural account of these miracles. They read and believe the record of how Jesus went about "preaching the gospel of the kingdom, and healing all manner of sickness and all manner of disease among the people"; how "they brought unto him all sick people that were taken with divers diseases and torments, and those which were possessed with devils, and those which were lunatic, and those that had the palsy; and he healed them" (Matt. 4:23, 24; 8:16, 17; 12:15; Mark 6:55, 56; Luke 4:40; 6:17–19; 9:10, 11).

Against the claim that these miracles of healing were intended by the Lord to continue only during the lifetime of the apostles, they present the promises, "These signs shall follow them that believe: In my name shall they cast out devils; they shall speak with new tongues; they shall take up serpents; and if they drink any deadly thing, it shall not hurt them; they shall lay hands on the sick, and they shall recover" (Mark 16:17, 18). "Verily, verily, I say unto you, He that believeth on me, the works that I do shall he do also; and greater works than these shall he do; because I go unto my Father" (John 14:12).

The Acts of the Apostles is a record of the fulfilment of these promises. "And by the hands of the apostles were many signs and wonders wrought among the people. . . . There came also a multitude out of the cities round about unto Jerusalem, bringing sick folks, and them which were vexed with unclean spirits; and they were healed every one" (Acts 5:12–16).

The claim that these miracles were confined to the ministry of the apostles is refuted by the records of the miracles by Philip and Stephen, members of the seven chosen to minister to the poor. Of the former it is recorded that "Philip went down to the city of Samaria, and preached Christ unto them. And the people with one accord gave heed unto those things which Philip spake, hearing and seeing the miracles which he did. For unclean spirits, crying with loud voice, came out of many that were possessed with them; and many taken with palsies, and that were lame, were healed. And there was great joy in that city" (Acts 8:5–8). Of the latter it is written that "Stephen, full of faith and power, did great wonders and miracles among the people" (Acts 6:8).

Thus we see that the promise that "these signs shall follow them that believe" appears in the *practice* of those who were not counted among the apostles. But not only does it appear in the practice of others besides the apostles, but by *precept* it is enjoined upon others of an order which, all will admit, continues as long as the church militant continues. Here is the precept: "Is any sick among you? let him call for the elders of the church; and let them pray over him, anointing him with oil in the name of the Lord; and the prayer of faith shall save the sick, and the Lord shall raise him up; and if he have committed sins, they shall be forgiven him. Confess your faults one to another, and pray one for another, that ye may be healed. The effectual fervent prayer of a righteous man availeth much" (James 5:14–16).

And the Lord, forseeing that the time would come when unbelief would attempt to relegate all miracles to the time of the fathers, and to attribute to them advantages not to be shared by other believers of a later time, calls special attention to the great miracle-working prophet Elias as "*a man subject to like passions as we are.*"

Notwithstanding these strong, unmistakable promises, the gift of healing is today practically absent from the church. If it were not, there would be no need of the advertising which is now so common. The multitudes cured would advertise so loudly that the healer would be thronged day and night, and possibly some earnest souls would tear the roof off the house in order to bring some sufferer into his presence. There are a few sick people who are healed even in this day of unbelief, but exercise of the gift of healing as witnessed in the days of Christ is nowhere seen.

When one reads the promises made to the church concerning healing and the wonderful record of miracles which were wrought in the early days of the church, and then contemplates the absence of these "mighty" works in the church of today, unless there is a clear understanding of the reason for it there will be heard Gideon's cry of staggered faith, "Where be all his miracles which our fathers told us of?" And there is danger that this will soon be followed by an attempt to limit miracles to the days of the apostles, and this in turn will be followed by the denial of all miracles, and this by the midnight of infidelity.

There is a reason for the absence of these gifts, but it is dangerous to one's reputation to give it. It used to be dangerous to life. As a result of giving this reason for the absence of miracles in Nazareth, our Lord was dragged down from the pulpit, out of the synagogue, to the edge of a precipice, down which the church leaders tried to dash Him to death (Luke 4:16–30). And what was this reason which wrought them up to such a rage? He told them, through references to similar conditions in the days of the prophets, that God could more safely manifest the gifts of healing on behalf of the heathen than He could on behalf of His church in their sinful unbelief. And herein lies the reason for the absence of these gifts today.

The church is backslidden. The Lord cannot honor a backslidden church. If He did, He would disgrace His throne. The world judges God by the lives of His people, and it is not inconsistent that it should; for the Lord has said of His people: "Ye are my witnesses," "Ye are the light of the world," "Ye are manifestly declared to be the epistle of Christ," "Ye are the body of Christ" (Isa. 43:12; Matt. 5:14; II Cor. 3:3; I Cor. 12:27). And the only way God has of saving His reputation when those who are sent forth as His witnesses witness against Him, is to *withhold His witness of approval from them* by no longer "bearing them witness, both with signs and wonders, and with divers miracles, and gifts of the Holy Ghost."

Should the Lord give the gifts of healing to some members of the church bearing His name today, whereby the world would be attracted to Him as it was to the apostles before the church had confessed its worldliness, it would only confirm that church in its worldliness and pride. The members of the church thus honored would meet the members of other communions with the exultant cry: "We are the true church! God has at last settled that question. Have you heard the news? God has placed in our church the gifts of healing, and the preaching of our creed is now confirmed with signs following. This proves that we are right and you are wrong."

Thus it is plainly seen that the withholding of the confirming miracles from the lukewarm church of today is the wisest thing the Lord can do. To do otherwise would be to confirm them in their opinion that they are "rich, and increased with goods, and have need of nothing," and close their ears to the message of God, on the acceptation of which hangs their salvation. "Thou art wretched, and miserable, and poor, and blind, and naked."

As I write, I praise God that He has not compromised His holiness by giving His confirming gifts to a backslidden church. I anticipate the song of vindication, sung on the sea of glass, when men shall come to see the wisdom and mercy of God in His dealings with the children of men: "Great and marvellous are thy works, Lord God Almighty; just and true are thy ways, thou King of saints" (Rev. 15:3).

CHAPTER THIRTY-SIX

THE GIFTS OF HEALING AND
GOD'S REPUTATION

Will the Lord withhold His gifts from one who is walking in the light, and who is wholly consecrated, and keep him back from manifesting the fulness of power because the church is backslidden? Most certainly He will. For Him to do otherwise would be to bring His truth and His name into disgrace. If those born blind or lame or dumb were being healed by the ministers of any worldly church today, that church would thereby be brought into great prominence, and every act of its members would be closely scrutinized as the acts of the people of the church whom God was approving by miracles and wonders and signs. And the God who gave the power for working these wonders and signs would be measured and judged by the sins of the people of the church thus prominently pointed out and honored.

But did not Christ, while a member of the Jewish church, perform His wonderful miracles of healing? Yes, but in order to save the reputation of God He was compelled to denounce the sins of the Jewish church, and finally to repudiate them before all the world.

The Jewish church claimed to be the only representatives on earth of the true God. They claimed this when they were more wicked than the Gentiles. When the Gentiles heard their claim and saw their crimes, they blasphemed. Paul says they did. They not only cursed the Jews, but they blasphemed the God of the Jews. This is not strange. The Jews claimed to be like Jehovah. The Gentiles, therefore, judged Jehovah by the Jews. They knew the Jews robbed widows and committed adultery. They knew the Jews did all this when they heard them making their long, loud prayers on the corners of the streets. This made them angry, and they blasphemed both the Jews and Jehovah. Paul presents it thus: "Thou, therefore, which teachest another, teachest thou not thyself? Thou that preachest a man should not steal, dost thou steal? Thou that sayest a man should not commit adultery, dost thou commit adultery? Thou that abhorrest idols, dost thou commit sacrilege? . . . For the name of God is blasphemed among the Gentiles through you" (Rom. 2:21-24).

Jesus came to save not only sinners, but the reputation of His Father. And in order to do this, He must tell the truth about His church. And He did. He declared in the hearing of the Gentiles that the leaders in the church were whited sepulchers—rotten at heart, were robbers of widows, pious hypocrites, a generation of vipers. When the Gentiles heard this, many stopped swearing at Jehovah. They saw that His professed church was misrepresenting Him. They listened to Christ's gracious words. When the Jews ordered them to arrest the Son of God, they refused and said, "Never man spake like this man."

Christ's miracles followed the cleansing of the temple. "And Jesus went into the temple of God, and cast out all them that sold and bought in the temple, and overthrew the tables of the moneychangers, and the seats of them that sold doves, and said unto them, It is written, My house shall be called the house of prayer; but ye have made it a den of thieves. And the blind and the lame came to him in the temple; and he healed them" (Matt. 21:12–14).

He could now perform His mighty cures without bringing honor to a dishonorable church and without bringing dishonor to Jehovah. By calling the Jewish church a den of thieves, Jesus was able to work miracles while a member of that church, without bringing disgrace upon His Father. But His faithfulness in rebuking the sins of His church cost Him not only His membership in that church, but His life.

The church of today is not free from its hypocrites and whited sepulchers. It is not free from its generation of vipers and its robbers of widows. And again the Gentiles blaspheme the name of God because of them. And again Jesus must come into the temple and cleanse it before it can again be written that "the blind and the lame came to him in the temple; and he healed them." Who will follow the example of Christ? Who will go into His pride-filled church, which he knows is full of unconverted men and women whose sins are a disgrace to the Christian name, and cry at its festivals and fairs and oyster suppers, "Babylon the great is fallen, is fallen, and is become the habitation of devils, and the hold of every foul spirit, and a cage of every unclean and hateful bird"? This is the first step for a consecrated man to take who is seeking the gift of healing while holding communion in a world-loving church. But this power to cast out devils may be purchased at the cost of his being cast out of his beloved synagogue, and finding a home with some humble church "everywhere spoken against." And from the church which will not be cleansed, Christ in the person of His true disciples will depart, uttering the fearful words, "Behold, your house is left unto you desolate."

But could not someone who is not a member of any church, who is consecrated, be instructed with the gifts of healing? No; for the gifts of the Spirit are given to the *church*, not to a disconnected, irresponsible individual. "God hath set some in the *church*, first apostles, secondarily prophets, thirdly teachers, after that miracles, then gifts of healings, helps, governments, diversities of tongues" (I Cor. 12:28). "The church of the living God" is "the pillar and ground of the truth" (I Tim. 3:15). It is not an invisible, intangible, irresponsible nonentity, but a real, tangible body made on purpose to be looked at: "Ye are the light of the world." It is also to be handled and read: "Ye are manifestly declared to be the epistle of Christ ministered by us, written not with ink, but with the Spirit of the living God; not in tables of stone, but in *fleshly tables of the heart*" (II Cor. 3:3). Of Christ it is written: "The Word was made flesh, and dwelt among us, and we beheld his glory" (John 1:14). But He has returned to His Father and we see Him no more except as we see Him in the flesh of the "church, which is his body, the fulness of him that filleth all in all."

No attempt was made by the glorious apostolic church to hide its literal organized existence, and thereby shirk the responsibility of the influence of unworthy members. It had power to cleanse itself from its Ananias and Sapphira, and to strike such terror to the hearts of the hypocrites on the outside that "of the rest durst no man join himself to them." This repudiation of church organization so common today is the swinging of the pendulum to the opposite extreme from the tyrannical organization of a fallen church. It is intended to escape the responsibility of church membership and the unpleasant duty of cleansing out those who "trespass" and who will not "hear the church" and repent of their sins (Matt. 18:15–17).

Yes, the absence of the confirming signs and wonders today is a solemn, silent, infallible proof of the presence of sin in the church. God is defending His honor from disgrace. He is withholding His witnessing wonders from a lukewarm church to save His reputation both in heaven and earth.

But how long shall this disgrace continue? How long shall God be compelled to testify against His church? When the unbeliever challenges the church to show the miracles which are plainly promised, we who believe the promises explain their absence on the ground of the presence of sin. But this is a disgraceful confession. It is a confession from the church that her relations with the world are such that her Head cannot fully identify himself with her without bringing himself into disgrace.

Who that reads these solemn truths will sense the sad situation and take the matter to heart? Reader, are you zealous for God's honor? Does the condition of the church concern you? Do you sigh and cry "for all the abominations that be done in the midst thereof"? Do you "weep between the porch and the altar," and cry, "Spare thy people, O Lord, and give not thine heritage to reproach"? Who will begin to cry to God for cleansing both for himself and the church, "and give him no rest, till he establish, and till he make Jerusalem a praise in the earth"? To this the writer has dedicated every power of body and mind. And I can bear testimony from personal experience to the fact that God will respond with His witnessing power just as fast as ministers and people are purged from the sins which separate them from the power of God.

CHAPTER THIRTY-SEVEN

CONFIRMING SIGNS

"That ye may know that the Son of man hath power on earth to forgive sins, . . . I say unto thee, Arise, and take up thy bed, and go thy way into thine house. And immediately he arose, took up the bed, and went forth before them all; insomuch that they were all amazed and glorified God, saying, We never saw it on this fashion" (Mark 2:10–12).

One important office of the gifts of the Spirit is to bear witness to the truthfulness of the word preached. Of the ministry of the Great Teacher, Peter spoke thus on the day of Pentecost: "A man *approved of God* among you *by miracles and wonders and signs*, which God did by him in the midst of you, as ye yourselves also know" (Acts 2:22).

Paul writes thus of the witnessing office of the gifts of the Spirit: "How shall we escape, if we neglect so great salvation; which at the first began to be spoken by the Lord, and was *confirmed* unto us by them that heard him; *God also bearing them witness*, both with *signs* and *wonders,* and with *divers miracles,* and *gifts of the Holy Ghost,* according to his own will?" (Heb. 2:3, 4).

"And they went forth, and preached everywhere, the Lord working with them, and *confirming the word with signs following*" (Mark 16:20). "Long time therefore they [Paul and Barnabas] tarried there [at Iconium], speaking boldly in the Lord, which *bare witness* unto the word of his grace, *granting signs and wonders to be done* by their hands" (Acts 14:3, R.V.).

The disciples understood the need of these confirming cures and witnessing wonders. We read how they prayed definitely for them, and how the Lord just as definitely gave them that which they asked. Here is the prayer:

"And now, Lord, behold their threatenings; and grant unto thy servants, that with all *boldness* they may *speak thy word,* by *stretching forth thine hand to heal;* and that *signs* and *wonders* may be done by the name of thy holy child Jesus. And when they had prayed, the place was shaken where they were assembled together; and they were all filled with the Holy Ghost, and they spake the word of God with boldness" (Acts 4:29–31).

Thus clearly do the Scriptures teach that the gifts of the Holy Ghost are given to *approve,* to *witness to,* and to *confirm* the preaching of the *Word.* The signs and wonders are not the things of greatest importance. The all-important thing is the *preaching of the Word.* The "signs and wonders," "divers miracles, and the gifts of the Holy Ghost" *follow* to *bear witness* that the *Word* spoken is the Word "which at the *first began to be spoken by the Lord.*"

The healing of the sick must, therefore, *follow* the preaching of the Word. "Preach the kingdom of God" and "heal the sick" is the order in which the commission is given. It is therefore evident that if the Word is not preached, God will not confirm it with signs following. For God to confirm the preaching of anything else but the Word would be for Him to confirm the preaching of a lie. If there is, therefore, any failure in the preaching of the Word, there must inevitably follow a failure in the signs following.

That there is a failure in the preaching of the Word today is plain to those who are not entirely blinded by the god of this world. Of this time the apostle Paul in his letter to Timothy wrote thus:

"I charge thee in the sight of God, and of Christ Jesus who shall judge the quick and the dead, and by his appearing and his kingdom: preach the *word...* For the time will come when they will not endure the sound doctrine; but, having itching ears, will heap to themselves teachers after their own lusts; and will turn away their ears from truth, and turn aside unto fables" (II Tim. 4:1–4, R.V.).

Will God confirm the preaching of fables? Then this falling away from the faith to fables is reason enough why God should refuse to confirm such preaching with signs following. Back to the Word, my brother, if you are seeking the witnessing signs. Back to the

Word which at the first began to be spoken by the Lord, before you begin to teach the fable that the witnessing signs and wonders were for the apostles only.

God working with them! What a blessed association in labor! "The Lord working with them, and confirming the word with signs following." What a glorious experience the early disciples must have had when the Lord worked with them confirming the Word! But why look back? He is the same yesterday, today, and forever. He will work with us again, confirming the Word, if the church will get back to that Word. For at the time He was working with them, confirming the Word with signs following, He promised His presence to us today when He said: "All power is given unto me in heaven and in earth. Go ye therefore, and teach all nations, baptizing them in the name of the Father, and of the Son, and of the Holy Ghost; teaching them to observe all things whatsoever I have commanded you; and, lo, I am with you alway, even unto the end of the world" (Matt. 28:18–20).

And for what will He be with us? To work with us, of course. And how does He work with us? It is by confirming the Word with signs following.

The absence, therefore, of the confirming signs is a sad and solemn witness to the fact that there is a failure somewhere in the preaching of the Word.

Reader, does this truth touch your heart? Does it make any difference to you whether the Lord works with the church and confirms the Word, or whether He does not? I confess that it concerns me deeply, and "for Zion's sake will I not hold my peace, and for Jerusalem's sake I will not rest, until the righteousness thereof go forth as brightness, and the salvation thereof as a lamp that burneth" (Isa. 62.1).

CHAPTER THIRTY-EIGHT

THE SWORD OF THE SPIRIT

He who is seeking the baptism with the Spirit is seeking to become the *sword* of the *Spirit*. Some have thought that they were to wield the Spirit as a *sword* is wielded in the hand of a mighty man. This is a wrong conception. On the contrary, the *Spirit* is to wield *us* and use *us* as a *sword*. But do not the Scriptures say that the sword of the Spirit is the *Word* of God? (Eph. 6:17). Yes, but it is the *"Word made flesh"* that is the Spirit's sword, and not the letter of the Word which is spoken by the self-righteous Pharisees who gather at the corner grocery and loaf and chew and smoke and "argue Scripture." No, no! The sword which the Spirit seeks to use is a human life upon which the Spirit has written the law of God, the Word of the Lord.

When the Lord was preparing to write His law on stone, He turned to Moses and said with intense longing, "O that there were such an *heart* in them, that they would fear me, and *keep all my commandments always*" (Deut. 5:29). This was but to say, O that I might write my law on my people's hearts instead of on these stones!

The reason why the Lord wrote the law on stone at Sinai was because He could not write it on the hearts of His people. From the day that He wrote His law on stone until this day, the Lord has been waiting for men to yield their hearts to Him that He might write the law there. This is the glory of the new covenant. "Behold, the days come, saith the Lord, that I will make a new covenant with the house of Israel, and with the house of Judah: not according to the covenant that I made with their fathers in the day that I took them by the hand to bring them out of the land of Egypt; which my covenant they brake, although I was an husband unto them, saith the Lord: but this shall be the covenant that I will make with the house of Israel; After those days saith the Lord, I will put my law in their inward parts, and write it in their hearts; and will be their God, and they shall by my people" (Jer. 31:31–33).

It was glorious when the Lord ministered the law to the yielding stone, but this glory is eclipsed in the glory which attends the ministering of this law to a yielded heart, whereby such a life becomes "the epistle of Christ" (a living letter of Christ addressed to sinful men), "written not with ink, but with the Spirit of the living God; not in tables of stone, but in fleshly tables of the heart" (II Cor. 3:1–8).

For centuries the Lord received only lip service from the great majority of His professed people. "This people draw near me with their mouth, and with their lips do honor me, but have removed their heart far from me, and their fear toward me is taught by the precept of men" (Isa. 29:13). There was plenty of form and ceremony, plenty of sacrifice and offering, but these from carnal hearts were only a weariness to the Lord, who wanted spiritual service from those upon whose hearts He had written His law (Isa. 1:14).

In the midst of all this heartless service—this yielding of the lips but not the life—a voice is heard saying: "Sacrifice and offering thou didst not desire; mine ears hast thou not opened; burnt offering and sin offering hast thou not required. Then said I, Lo, I come; in the volume of the book it is written of me, I delight to do thy will, O my God; yea, *the law is within my heart*" (Ps. 40:6–8).

The apostle Paul quotes this Scripture in Hebrews 10, and applies it to Christ with this additional thought: "Sacrifice and offering thou wouldest not, but a *body* hast thou prepared me." This was the promise of Christ that He would come to the world in human flesh and show to the world what His Father desired in men, that He desired a body, a living man, in whom and through whom He might display the glories of His Word. In fulfilment of His promise He came, and this is the record which the apostle John bears of His coming: "In the beginning was the Word, and the Word was with God, and the Word was God." "And the *Word was made flesh*, and dwelt among us." "In him was life; and the *life* was the *light* of men."

In Jesus, the Word made flesh, the Spirit held a perfect sword, and consequently there was no limiting or measuring of the power by which the Spirit used this sword for righteousness against sin.

It is not enough to *say* the truth; we must *be* the truth. Christ said, "I *am* . . . the *truth*." Again, "I *am* . . . the *life*." "The words that I speak unto you, they are spirit, and they are life"; and this because He spake only that which He *lived*. His words were words of *truth* and *life*, because He spake those words which were *true* in His *life*, words which were made flesh, words which were translated into acts. And herein lay the difference between His speaking and the speaking of the Pharisees. The Lord says, "They *say* and *do* not." He first *did* that which He *said;* consequently He spake as one having authority, and not as the scribes.

God has no truth for the world that He wants given in *theory*. "Sacrifice and offering thou wouldest not, but a body hast thou prepared me." "Burnt offering and sin offering hast thou not required. Then said I, Lo, I come; . . . I delight to do thy will, O my God, yea, thy law is within my heart."

Reader, if you have a theory of a truth which you want your neighbors to accept, first furnish that truth with a *body*, with *your* body. Truth without a body in which to manifest itself is dead, being alone. And this is what James means when he says, "So *speak* ye, and so *do*, as they that shall be judged by the law of liberty." That he has in mind the translation of the truth into the life, the translation of the faith into flesh, is clear from what follows: "If a brother or sister be naked, and destitute of daily food, and one of you say unto them, Depart in peace, be ye warmed and filled; notwithstanding ye give them not those things which are needful to the body; what doth it profit? Even so *faith*, if it hath not *works*, is dead, being alone."

Again I repeat, if you have a theory of a truth that you want your family and friends to receive, first let that truth be written on your heart by the Holy Spirit. Then you will become that truth made flesh, so that your family and neighbors will have a chance to see the truth when they look at you, to hear the truth when they hear you, and to handle the truth when they shake hands with you. This is what the apostle John means when he writes of our Lord thus:

"That which was from the beginning, which we have heard, which we have seen with our eyes, which we have looked upon, and our hands have handled, of the Word of life (for the life was manifested, and we have seen it, and bear witness, and show unto you that eternal life, which was with the Father, and was manifested unto us)" (I John 1:1, 2).

Do you believe in the "blessed hope" of the second coming of our Lord and Saviour Jesus Christ? Do you want your neighbors to believe this truth? Then let that blessed hope live in your life, yes, *be* that blessed hope made flesh, so that your neighbors will fall in love with it by falling in love with your blessed life, which has been made blessed by the blessed hope.

Do you want your neighbors to love that law which by the new covenant is written upon the heart? Then let it be written upon your heart. Furnish it a body. Let it be made flesh in your life, and thereby become "holy and just and good," as the law appeared when made flesh, when written within the heart of the Son of God.

Reader, of these things here written this is the sum:
The Lord wants you to bring the Word which you profess, into the inner sanctuary of your heart. He wants
your body in which to display to the world what His
gospel will do for a sinful man. He wants His Word
made flesh again in your life. He wants you to be a
walking Bible before you are a *talking* Bible. He wants
you to walk worthy of the high calling before you talk
wisely of it. The letter killeth, but the Spirit maketh
alive. This spiritless talking about the letter of the
Word, that which is contradicted by the life of the talk-
er, is what is killing the cause of Christianity in the
world today. Let the reader know assuredly that the
Holy Spirit will not baptize with power for witnessing
that man or woman whose words of witness are contradicted by the walk of life. If you are seeking for the
Spirit without measure as experienced by the great
Example and Teacher of the new covenant, then you
must be as He was, the Word of God made flesh.

It is shocking to hear men and women talk of being
baptized with the Holy Ghost while their lives are anything but the light of the world, and while they are
ignorant of the Word and show no real desire to study
it and have it built into their lives. I want to witness
right here, with all the earnestness of my being, to the
truth that I am unable to speak with power from on
high *any words but those of the Scriptures of truth*,
and no words from the Scriptures of truth except *those
words which have been made flesh and dwelt in my
life.*

The thing which is the greatest enemy of the gospel of the kingdom today is the preaching of a faith

that is not made flesh, the teaching of a law that is not in the life, the teaching of a truth that is not traced on the tablets of the heart. This is what turns the world from the truth. This is what causes the Gentiles to blaspheme today as they did in the days of Paul. Here is God's estimate of that preaching of the Word which is not in the life: "Thou therefore which teachest another, teachest thou not thyself? thou that preachest a man should not steal, dost thou steal? thou that sayest a man should not commit adultery, dost thou commit adultery? thou that abhorrest idols, dost thou commit sacrilege? thou that makest thy boast of the law, through breaking the law dishonourest thou God? For the *name of God is blasphemed among the Gentiles through you*, as it is written" (Rom. 2:21–24). Then search the Scriptures as you never have done before. You can have the Spirit of truth to guide you into all truth. Having found the truth, then let the Spirit write it upon the tables of your heart that He may make you a sword of the Spirit; and then, and not till then, can you hope to be wielded by the Spirit with Pentecostal power. "Receive with meekness the engrafted word." "Be partakers of the divine nature." "Receive ye the Holy Ghost."

CHAPTER THIRTY-NINE

"WHY MARVEL YE AT THIS?"

Before the Lord can restore the gifts of healing to His servants today, they must reach the place in their experience where they will not get excited at the manifestation of signs and wonders which are wrought to confirm the Word. And the only man or woman who will be calm in the presence of miracles of healing is the man or woman who is in possession of the power of God to save from sinning. The reason for this is that he who is kept by the power of God unto salvation is perpetually in the presence of the crowning miracle of the gospel. All other miracles are inferior to this miracle. All other miracles are servants to this miracle. All the miraculous gifts of the Spirit will fail "when that which is perfect is come," but this miracle will never fail (I Cor. 13:1–10). This crowning miracle will be exhibited by our Lord to be admired by all the universe, in all "the ages to come," as the glorious manifestation of the exceeding riches of His grace.

"And you hath he quickened, who were dead in trespasses and sins; wherein in time past ye walked according to the course of this world, according to the prince of the power of the air, the spirit that now work-eth in the children of disobedience, among whom also we all had our conversation in times past in the lusts of our flesh, fulfiling the desires of the flesh and of the mind; and were by nature the children of wrath, even as others. But God, who is rich in mercy, for his great love wherewith he loved us, even when we were dead in sins, hath quickened us together with Christ (by grace are ye saved); and hath raised us up together, and made us sit together in heavenly places in Christ Jesus; that in the ages to come he might show the exceeding riches of his grace in his kindness toward us through Christ Jesus" (Eph. 2:1–7).

How can that man or that woman who is in possession of such an experience as this, who has thus been resurrected from the dead, who is constantly kept alive by the "power of his resurrection" and is constantly experiencing this miracle of all miracles, get excited at beholding another miracle which is only the handmaid of this one?

This point is sometimes made in order to evade the demand for the lesser miracles. But be assured it is not so made here. It is presented here to clear the King's highway for the manifestation of all the miracles and wonders and signs which followed to confirm the Word in the apostolic days of purity and power.

This running away from the gospel, which is the power of God unto salvation, after the less important signs and wonders is a sad but certain witness that all who do it have not yet been anointed with the Holy

Ghost, whereby they are able rightly to compare spiritual things with spiritual.

Before the day of Pentecost, the Lord sent out seventy disciples with the commission to "heal the sick" "and say unto them, The kingdom of God is come nigh unto you." From the report which they gave when they returned, it was apparent that they were in danger of losing sight of the gospel of the kingdom, and running away after miracles of less importance. They said nothing of the progress of the gospel of the kingdom, but spoke of the miracles they were able to perform.

"And the seventy returned again with joy, saying, Lord, even the devils are subject unto us through thy name." To which the Lord answered in gentle reproof: "Behold, I give unto you power to tread on serpents and scorpions, and over all the power of the enemy; and nothing shall by any means hurt you. Notwithstanding in this rejoice not, that the spirits are subject unto you; but rather rejoice, because your names are written in heaven" (Luke 10:17-20).

The climax by which this crowning miracle is reached is presented thus by Jesus in the sign to John the Baptist that Christ was "he that should come": "Go your way, and tell John what things ye have seen and heard; how that the blind see, the lame walk, the lepers are cleansed, the deaf hear, the dead are raised. to the poor the gospel is preached" (Luke 7:22).

After Pentecost, the apostles never failed to give these miracles their proper importance. All the miracles of that day only opened the way for the cry, "Repent, and be baptized every one of you in the name of Jesus

Christ for the remission of sins, and ye shall receive the gift of the Holy Ghost" (Acts 2:38). When the cripple was healed at the Beautiful Gate and all the people were "amazed" and "ran together unto them," "greatly wondering," Peter said: "Ye men of Israel, why marvel ye at this?" "Repent ye therefore, and be converted" (Acts 3:1–19). And to the rulers he said: "Ye rulers of the people, and elders of Israel, if we this day be examined of the good deed done to the impotent man, by what means he is made whole; be it known unto you all, and to all the people of Israel, that by the name of Jesus Christ of Nazareth, whom ye crucified, whom God raised from the dead, even by him doth this man stand here before you whole.... Neither is there salvation in any other; for there is none other name under heaven given among men, whereby we must be saved" (Acts 4:8–12).

Notwithstanding, "God wrought special miracles by the hands of Paul," but we do not find either in his epistles or sermons as recorded in the Acts of the Apostles any attempt to make prominent these miracles of healing. He did refer to them in a general way; but even then it was done largely to confirm his apostle-ship which was questioned by certain "false brethren"; and then he did it reluctantly. "Christ, and him cruci-fied" was his message everywhere, to which he oft added, as his personal testimony, the story of the mir-acle of his conversion.

From all this it is clear that before God can work with us, confirming the Word with signs following, we must experience the miracle of all miracles, salvation from sin and sinning, and hold that miracle *in our hearts*, and in *the hearing of the multitude*, high above all miracles which are granted to confirm this, the chief of miracles. Then this great barrier to the coming of the confirming miracles will be cleared away.

To this I wish to bear witness by relating an experience which came under my observation. A young minister was associated with others in gospel labor at a large religious gathering. A few sick people were healed in connection with the preaching of the Word. He had never seen it on this wise before, and he was much stirred by this manifestation of God's healing power. He preceded the other ministers to the next appointment and immediately began to call attention to the miracles of healing which he had witnessed. Soon the congregation was all absorbed with the theme of physical healing. At this point he visited a barber shop and contracted the barber's itch, which soon manifested itself in large sores on his neck, so located as to be in plain view. "How can I preach healing, and pray with the sick, while thus afflicted myself?" he reasoned. "Will not the people say, 'Physician, heal thyself'? I must be healed." Prayer was offered, and although one person present was instantly healed, he was not. This was the situation when the other ministers arrived. The young man, with great concern, related this experience and asked why he was not healed. Not being acquainted with the course he had pursued, they could not explain his disappointment. The next day he came to them, his face beaming with the light of a new truth which had dawned upon him. He said in substance: "Now I understand. Now the Lord can heal. I made the mistake of calling the attention of the people to miracles of healing, when they needed first to be healed of their sinning." Not only did he make this private acknowledgment of his error, but he made a voluntary public confession to the same effect. Prayer was again offered, and he was healed and made happy with the truth thus emphasized that the healing of the soul from sin is the first great miracle, which the Lord would have impressed upon His sinning people.

This grand truth, if experienced by ministers and people in the church of God, will not only clear the King's highway for the manifestation of the fulness of the promised power, but it will save all who believe it from being deceived by the "all power and signs and lying wonders" which are predicted, and which are already appearing, to deceive, if it were possible, the very elect.

Who that reads these lines will yield himself to the miracle of God's saving and keeping power? And then, in the joyful possession of this miracle, and with it an unquenchable longing to bear it to others, who will continue to pray for those "mighty signs and wonders, by the power of the Spirit of God," which wrought in the early days of purity and power, "to make the Gentiles obedient" to the Gospel? (Rom. 15: 18, 19). To this end these lines are penned.

Another witness by letter:

"I am only too glad to tell you that the anchor holds. More than that, it is going to hold, for I have given myself and all I ever expect to be to Christ, and so I cannot fail. The Bible is the most wonderful book in the world. I have just begun to learn how to study it. I never expected to see any miracle performed, but I think it was a greater miracle to straighten me up than it was to straighten that crooked woman spoken of in Luke 13:11; and more, too, because I had been in sin three years longer than she had been under the power of disease. I praise God for His keeping power. Praise God for the power that can keep anyone from smoking, swearing, and out of bad company!"

CHAPTER FORTY

MIRACLES OF HEALING AND HEALTH REFORM.
SALVATION FOR THE BODY

The gospel includes sanctification of the *body*. "And the very God of peace sanctify you *wholly*," says the Word. And the next sentence explains what is meant by being "wholly" sanctified: "And I pray God your whole spirit and soul and *body be preserved blameless* unto the coming of our Lord Jesus Christ" (I Thess. 5:23).

Sanctification is complete salvation from sin. "Thou shalt call his name Jesus; for he shall save his people *from their sins*" (Matt. 1:21). The salvation of Jesus, therefore, includes the salvation of the spirit, soul, and *body from sin*. It is possible, therefore, to sin against the body. "Know ye not that your *body* is the temple of the Holy Ghost which is in you, which ye have of God, and ye are not your own? For ye are bought with a price; therefore glorify God in your *body*," which is His (I Cor. 6:19, 20). "If any man defile the temple of God, him shall God destroy; for the temple of God is holy, which temple ye are" (I Cor. 3:17). God must, therefore, save us from sinning against, or defiling the *body*, since our bodies must be presented blameless at the coming of our Lord Jesus Christ.

But how is sanctification for the body accomplished? How may we present our bodies blameless at the coming of our Lord Jesus Christ? By the same process and by the same power by which the soul is presented blameless. Complete sanctification of the soul is accomplished by completely separating the soul from sin. But God does not separate a soul from sin without that soul's *knowledge* and *consent*. How could He? How could I be saved from committing a sin which I did not know to be a sin? If I do not know it to be wrong, I must of necessity think it right. How can God save me from doing that which is sin while I consider it to be righteousness, or right doing? It is, therefore, plain that God must first show me that the thing is sin before I can be saved from it. This is Bible sanctification. "Sanctify them through thy truth; thy word is truth" (John 17:17). Perfect sanctification, therefore, necessitates a perfect knowledge of the truth; or in other words, a perfect knowledge of the Word, for "thy word is truth."

Thus it is plain that God cannot sanctify a sinner while the sinner continues sinning. He cannot sanctify sin. All this applies to the sanctification of the body. God cannot sanctify the body, or save the body from sin, cannot heal it or restore it to a blameless body, without first pointing out those physical sins which defile or destroy the body.

Should the Lord heal, or sanctify, the body before the cause of the sickness is pointed out and put away, He would, in the healing, supply His own strength to the transgressor to be used in further transgression. He would be saving the transgressor against the laws of health, *in* his sins and not *from* his sins. Not only this, but He would make it impossible ever to save the sinner from his sins. For if the transgressor was continually saved from the results of his transgression, he would never know the seriousness of transgression, nor realize the necessity of ceasing to transgress. The health which God gave would be consumed on his appetites and pleasures, and thus God would be furnishing His miraculous power to be used in violating the laws of life and health. This would make Christ a minister of sin. "Is therefore Christ the minister of sin? God forbid" (Gal. 2:17).

To illustrate: One is made sick and kept sick by wrong habits or sins in eating, or drinking, or dressing, or working. In order to save the sinner from his sins, the Lord points out the sin and calls for a reform; but the reform calls for self-denial, which the transgressor is unwilling to make because it conflicts with his appetite, or pride, or ambitions. He continues to grieve the Spirit by transgression, yet asks prayer for healing. He asks that the Holy Spirit, which pointed out the sin, be manifested to heal while he uses this added health to add to his transgressions. By this course he virtually says to the Lord: "I want to be saved from the results of sinning, but I do not want to stop sinning. I know that my sickness is the result of wrong habits of life, but I want to be healed so that I may live and continue in sin. I don't want to be saved *from* sin; I want to be saved *in* sin."

From all this, it is plain that for God to heal the body without pointing out the transgressions against the body which are responsible for the sickness, would be to nullify the whole plan of salvation, which is to save the people *from* their sins, not *in* their sins.

He who teaches sanctification for the soul and does not point out the sins of the soul and call for a separation from sin, is not working in harmony with the gospel plan of salvation. Likewise, he who professes to heal the body and does not point out the sins against the body—those wrong habits of life which are responsible for sickness—and present the gospel of salvation from these sins, is not working in harmony with Jesus Christ, the Author of our salvation. For He said to the man whom He had healed at the pool of Bethesda, "Behold, thou art made whole; *sin no more, lest a worse thing come unto thee*" (John 5:14).

This truth constitutes one of the infallible tests by which the true and false teachers of healing are to be tested. It is not the only test, but it is an important one, and if applied today, will brand as false a multitude of persons professing to possess the power to heal.

A widely advertised "great healer" stood on the streets of one of our large cities. A multitude was flocking to him to be healed. His beard was trimmed to resemble the purported pictures of the Son of God. I went near to hear and see. I saw him pressing his fingers on the patient's spine and looking up to heaven, but no sins were pointed out and no gospel of salvation from sin was proclaimed.

Reader, be not deceived. "By their fruits ye shall know them." "Preach the kingdom of God" and "heal the sick" is the commission from Him whom God sent "to bless you, in turning away every one of you from his iniquities" (Acts 3:26).

The presence of so much that is false pleads eloquently for the presence of the true. Let every soul who holds the prosperity of truth above his chief joy cease not to pray until the "all power" in heaven and in earth shall be revealed to meet the "all power and signs and lying wonders" which are appearing in these last days.

CHAPTER FORTY-ONE

LYING WONDERS

It is the plan of the enemy of all truth to counterfeit every manifestation of the power of God, and through that counterfeit to deceive the world and lead it to destruction.

According to the Scriptures of truth, this counterfeiting of the work of God is to reach its climax of power to deceive and destroy, in the closing events of the last days. That Satan through his agents will work miracles and signs and wonders to deceive, and that this work of deception is to be especially manifest in the last days, is plainly proved by the following Scriptures:

"Whose coming is after the working of Satan with all power and signs and lying wonders, and with all deceivableness of unrighteousness in them that perish; because they received not the love of the truth, that they might be saved" (II Thess. 2:9, 10). "And he deceiveth them that dwell on the earth by the means of those miracles which he had power to do" (Rev. 13:14). "For they are the spirits of devils, working miracles, which go forth unto the kings of the earth and of the whole world, to gather them to the battle of that great day of God Almighty" (Rev. 16:14). "There shall arise false Christs, and false prophets, and shall show great signs and wonders; insomuch that if it were possible, they shall deceive the very elect. Behold, I have told you before" (Matt. 24:24, 25).

From these startling statements of divine truth, it is clear that a correct understanding of the Scriptures concerning miracles is of vital importance. First of all it is all-important that he who would not be deceived must believe that the agents of Satan have power to "show great signs and wonders" and "miracles," as the above Scriptures plainly declare. And here is the reason: When Satan does perform great signs and wonders and miracles, the man who does not believe the declaration of our Lord that Satan has power to do so, will attribute the miracles to the power of God. How could he be worse deceived than to believe that the power and work of Satan is the power and work of God?

A correct understanding of what is meant by the term "miracle" in this connection is essential. From our standpoint a miracle, or sign, or wonder is any manifestation of power which we cannot explain at the working of what we call natural law. It may be wrought in harmony with the laws of nature; but if it is in a field of nature beyond our knowledge of the natural, it is to us *super*natural, i.e., above our knowledge of the natural.

Satan, under the symbol of the "king of Tyrus," is described by the prophet as sealing "up the sum, full of wisdom," and as having once held the position of the "anointed cherub that covereth." This position, according to Exodus 25:17–22 and Psalm 80:1, is one of two positions nearest the throne of God. Is it not reasonable to conclude that the one who is now called "the god of this world" (II Cor. 4:4) and "the *prince* of the *power* of the *air*" (Eph. 2:2) should be acquainted with forces of nature not known to man? Christ and His apostles made use of "miracles and wonders and signs" to show the power of God and advance His kingdom. Then is it to be wondered at that Satan and his followers should use their power and knowledge to do "great signs and wonders" to deceive the world and advance the kingdom of darkness?

It is not contended that Satan is able to do the *same* miracles which our Lord and His disciples performed, but only that he performs *similar miracles*. While they are not the same, they are nevertheless *miracles*, the manifestation of *supernatural* power; and so far as *men* are able to judge, they will appear to be the *same miracles*.

Inasmuch as the Word plainly declares that Satan will work miracles to deceive, and since all miracles are, so far as men are concerned, supernatural and therefore beyond our power to explain, it follows that it is unwise to *investigate miracles* for the purpose of ascertaining their *author*. No one who is instructed in the Scriptures *will ever attempt to determine the author of a miracle by investigating the miracle*. All that the miracle shows, standing alone, is the presence of supernatural power.

While the authorship of miracles cannot be determined by examining the miracles, yet there is a way by which it can be determined. Here is the test:

"Beware of false prophets, which come to you in sheep's clothing, but inwardly they are ravening wolves. *Ye shall know them by their fruits.* Do men gather grapes of thorns, or figs of thistles? Even so every good tree bringeth forth good fruit; but a corrupt tree bringeth forth evil fruit. A good tree cannot bring forth evil fruit, *neither can a corrupt tree bring forth good fruit. . . . Wherefore by their fruits ye shall know them*" (Matt. 7:15-20).

It will be noticed that the Lord does not say, "Ye shall know them by their 'great signs and wonders.' " but, "Ye shall know them by their *fruits.*" We are therefore to discern the author of miracles by the fruits and not by the miracles. This important truth was first taught by the Lord to the Israelites, thus:

"If there arise among you a prophet, or a dreamer of dreams, and giveth thee a sign or a wonder, and *the sign or the wonder come to pass,* whereof he spake unto thee, saying, *Let us go after other gods,* which thou hast not known, and let us serve them; thou shalt not hearken unto the words of that prophet, or that dreamer of dreams; for the Lord your God proveth you, to know whether ye love the Lord your God with all your heart and with all your soul. Ye shall walk after the Lord your God, and fear him, and keep his commandments, and obey his voice, and ye shall serve him, and cleave unto him. And that prophet, or that dreamer of dreams, shall be put to death" (Deut. 13:1-5).

It will be noted again that the Lord does not instruct us to investigate the miracle. He himself admits the fact that a miracle has been wrought, but He instructs us to investigate the teaching and the fruits which accompany the miracle.

Just as there is a distinction in the gospel system between the "gifts of the Spirit" and the "fruit of the Spirit," so there is a difference in the miraculous *powers* of the "spirits of devils" and the *fruits* of their teaching. While the miracles are beyond our power to judge, the fruits are not. While Satan will successfully counterfeit miracles, as he did at the court of Pharaoh, he cannot counterfeit the fruits of the Spirit. Reader, remember this truth if you would be delivered from the delusions of the last days: Don't investigate the miracle. *Admit the miracle, and challenge the fruits.*

Those who finally escape deception by "those miracles which he had power to do" will be men and women who are so fortified by what the Lord has told them before in the Scriptures that they will stand unmoved in the presence of "great signs and wonders," in the presence of the "working of Satan with all power and signs and lying wonders," and will refuse that teaching which is supported by the great signs and wonders wrought by Satan.

Let it be here understood that the miracles of Satan are but a means to an end. Just as the signs and wonders of Christ were wrought to confirm the word of truth, the gospel of salvation, so the signs and wonders of Satan are wrought to confirm the teaching of error, the doctrines of destruction.

Not only must those who escape the deceptions of Satan refuse to accept error though it be supported by great signs and wonders, but they must reject the error even when the signs and wonders that appear in support of it are wrought by those professing to be Christians, and whose *outward appearance* cannot be distinguished from that of the *genuine Christian*. Our Saviour says, "Beware of false prophets, which come to you in *sheep's clothing,* but inwardly they are ravening wolves." The term "sheep" stands in the Scriptures for true Christians. "Sheep's clothing," therefore, in this connection, must mean that the deceivers will bear the *outward* appearance of *genuine Christians*. This the apostle Paul plainly teaches in the following Scripture:

"For such men are false apostles, deceitful workers, fashioning themselves into apostles of Christ. And no marvel; for even Satan fashioneth himself into an angel of light. It is no great thing therefore if his ministers also fashion themselves as ministers of righteousness" (II Cor. 11:13–15, R.V.).

But not only will the ministers of Satan fashion themselves into ministers of righteousness in all their outward appearance while working great signs and wonders, but these signs and wonders will be wrought in the *name of Christ*. "For many shall come *in my name*, saying, I am Christ; and shall deceive many" (Matt. 24:5). "Many will say to me in that day, Lord, Lord, have we not prophesied *in thy name?* and *in thy name* have cast out devils? and *in thy name* done many wonderful works? And then will I profess unto them, I never knew you; depart from me, ye that work iniquity" (Matt. 7:22, 23).

If these workers did not believe that they had really cast out devils and done many wonderful works in the name of Christ, they would not presume to face Him with such self-justifying questions. The startling truth now clearly before us is this: the ministers of Satan will not only work miracles, but they will perform them with all the outward appearance of ministers of right-eousness—perform them in the sincere belief that they are *really casting out devils, and really doing wonder-ful works with the power and approval of Jesus Christ.*

Therefore, he who would escape being deceived by the overmastering deceptions of the last days, must be prepared to stand unmoved in the presence of one who lays his hands on the sick and, with the firm belief in himself that he is a minister of righteousness, a disciple of Christ, but is not, calls on the God of heaven in the name of Christ to manifest His Holy Spirit and heal. He must be unmoved by that which to all ap-pearances is a wonderful miracle of healing, which the professed minister believes to be a miracle, and which the patient believes to be a miracle wrought by the mighty power of God. "Who shall be able to stand!"

There are several searching questions which arise at this point. One of them is, How is it that a man can be so deceived that he really believes he is a minister of righteousness when he is the minister of Satan? This and other related questions will be answered in the next chapter.

CHAPTER FORTY-TWO

DECEIVING AND BEING DECEIVED

It is sad indeed to contemplate the fact that many will come to judgment so deceived that they will really believe that they have prophesied, cast out devils, and done many wonderful works in the name of Christ (Matt. 7:22, 23). The reason for their deception is plainly stated in the Scriptures. "In the last days perilous times shall come. For men shall be lovers of their own selves, covetous, boasters, proud, . . . lovers of pleasures more than lovers of God; having a form of godliness, but denying the power thereof. . . . Now as Jannes and Jambres withstood Moses, so do these also resist the *truth;* men of corrupt minds, reprobate concerning the *faith.* . . . Evil men and seducers shall wax worse and worse, deceiving, and *being deceived*" (II Tim. 3:1–13).

In the fourth chapter of II Timothy, which is but a continuation of the thought in the third, the apostle Paul explains more clearly how men reach that condition where they become victims of such terrible self-deception. Here is the reason: "I charge thee therefore before God, and the Lord Jesus Christ, who shall

239

judge the quick and the dead at his appearing and his kingdom; *preach the word*; be instant in season, out of season; reprove, rebuke, exhort with all longsuffering and *doctrine*. For the time will come when they will *not endure sound doctrine*; but after their own lusts shall they heap to themselves teachers, having itching ears; *and they shall turn away their ears from the truth*, and shall be turned unto fables" (II Tim. 4:1–4).

The apostle completes the description of their deception in these words: "Whose coming is after the working of Satan with all power and signs and lying wonders, and with all deceivableness of unrighteousness in them that perish; *because they received not the love of the truth*, that they might be saved. And for this cause God shall send them strong delusion, that they should believe a lie; that they all might be damned *who believed not the truth*, but had pleasure in unrighteousness" (II Thess. 2:9–12).

These Scriptures make the matter very plain. The only means which God has for saving man from error and the delusions of Satan is by the truth—"Thy word is truth"—by the sound doctrine of the Scriptures of truth. And when men will not receive the love of the truth, but have pleasure in unrighteousness; when they will not endure sound doctrine, but turn away their ears from the truth and listen to fables, there is nothing left that God can do but permit them to be deceived by the strong delusions which must result from following fables. No man will come to the judgment self-deceived who has not at some time in his experience stood face to face with truth. And because that truth called for self-denial, *as truth always does*, and because that truth was unpopular, *as truth always is*, he turned his ear away from the truth to the fables of false prophets. Instead of believing the truth, he came to believe a lie.

Reader, if you have come face to face with the truth, and turned away your ear from hearing it at any time in your life, I exhort you in the name of the Lord, delay not to turn your ear back to hear that truth and obey it at any cost. Let no honest seeker after truth fear that God will not be able to pilot him amid the hidden rocks and destructive quicksands which must be passed before we reach the haven. The Lord has promised that "if any man willeth to do his will, he shall know the doctrine."

A knowledge of sound doctrine is essential if the believer would be delivered from the delusions of the last days. *The signs and wonders of the ministers of Satan are wrought to persuade the people to believe false doctrine.* In *sound doctrine* there is salvation from false doctrines. Here is an illustration: there is one sound doctrine of Scripture which, if believed, would instantly sweep away a multitude of deceptions. One lie which the signs and wonders of Satan are wrought to confirm is that Christ's second coming will not occur in the manner described in the Scriptures. The Lord tells us that the workers of signs and wonders will teach false doctrine concerning the *manner* of His coming, and warns us not to believe them. Here is the Scripture:

"There shall arise false Christs, and false prophets, and shall show great signs and wonders; insomuch that, if it were possible, they shall deceive the very elect. Behold, I have told you before. Wherefore if they shall say unto you, Behold, he is in the desert, go not forth; behold, he is in the secret chambers, believe it not. For as the lightning cometh out of the east, and shineth even unto the west; *so shall also the coming of the Son of man be*" (Matt. 24:24–27).

This sound doctrine, if believed, would quickly unmask both the miracle-working delusions, Christian Science and Spiritualism; for both of them are saying, "Here is Christ," and denying His literal, personal coming in the clouds of heaven as described in the Scriptures of truth.

With the plain declarations of Christ as to the manner of His coming, what excuse will any man have in the judgment for having believed the fables of Christian Science or Spiritualism, even though these fables were supported by great signs and wonders? Do not the Scriptures of truth warn us beforehand that great signs and wonders will be wrought by those who will teach error concerning the second coming of Christ? The presence of miracles, therefore, is no excuse for being deceived. Miracles are to be judged by their fruits as to whether these fruits are in harmony with sound doctrine. This truth is taught all through the Scriptures. The prophet Isaiah, after describing a last-day delusion under which men leave the all-wise God and seek the dead for knowledge, admonishes the people to test the teaching and the miracles by sound doctrine. "To the law and to the testimony; if they speak not according to this word, it is because there is no light in them" (Isa. 8:19, 20). With this explicit warning before us, what excuse will any man have for being ruined by these delusions?

In Revelation 13:14 we read that the ministers of Satan deceive "them that dwell on the earth by the means of these miracles which he had power to do." Of those who escape this deception we read, "Here are they that keep the commandments of God, and the faith of Jesus" (Rev. 14:12). Thus it is again that the appeal of the undeceived will be to sound doctrine, and if the fruit of the teaching leads away from "the commandments of God, and the faith of Jesus," it will not be followed, notwithstanding the "miracles which he had the power to do."

In Matthew 7:22 we learn the awfully sad fact that men will come to judgment really believing that they have prophesied and cast out devils in the name of Christ. But the preceding verse gives the reason, as follows: "Not every one that saith unto me, Lord, Lord, shall enter into the kingdom of heaven; but he that *doeth the will of my Father* which is in heaven." Thus again the reason for the deception is found in the failure to do the will of God as taught in the Scriptures. Those who obey the Word have the following precious promises: "Because thou hast kept the word of my patience, I also will keep thee from the hour of temptation, which shall come upon all the world, to try them that dwell upon the earth" (Rev. 3:10). "My sheep hear my voice, and I know them, and they follow me; and I give unto them eternal life; and they shall never perish, neither shall any man pluck them out of my hand" (John 10:27, 28). "Fear not, little flock; for it is your Father's good pleasure to give you the kingdom" (Luke 12:32).

It has been asked, Will Satan really heal? Will the ministers of Satan cast out devils? Does Satan cast out Satan? It can be confidently affirmed from the teaching of Scripture that Satan will never cast out Satan, for this would be breaking his dominion over the soul, and he will never be found doing this. But it is evident that his ministers will do that which will appear to be casting out devils. There are many ways by which Satan exercises his control over men. The Pharisees were as much under the dominion of Satan as were those out of whom the Lord cast the devils. He said of them, "Ye are of your father the devil, and the lusts of your father ye will do" (John 8:44).

The devil can *change the manner* of his control and still retain power over his victim. Thereby he strengthens his deceptions not only over the victim, but over those who regard the miracle as a manifestation of the power of God in casting out devils. Here is an illustration: A man was trying to convince the writer that Spiritualism was a blessing. In support of his contention, he declared that he had been saved from drunkenness by means of Spiritualism. "As a result you are now a confirmed Spiritualist?" I asked; to which he answered, "Yes." "Now," I added, "you are harder to reach with the truth than if you were a drunkard."

In the same way Satan will appear to heal disease and cast out devils, and so far as the manifestation itself is concerned, it will be impossible to deny that a miracle has been wrought. But there will be no real deliverance from his dominion; only a shifting of symptoms, a change in the manner of control, whereby he will be able to deepen his deception. It is true that many of the wonders of healing can be accounted for on the psychological truth that the mind has much to do with the healing of the body. But, as before stated, the appeal is not to miracles, but to the fruits of the teaching in support of which the miracles are set forth. Miracles which cannot be denied, and which cannot be accounted for in harmony with the known laws of nature, will be wrought, and it is not wise to investigate the miracle. *Admit the miracle and challenge the fruits.* "By their fruits ye shall know them."

But since we are to know them by their fruits, it follows that *we must know the fruits when we see them.* If we cannot recognize coveting in ourselves, we will not know it in the worker of wonders. "I had not known coveting," says the apostle Paul, "except the law had said, Thou shalt not covet" (Rom. 7:7, R.V.). "By the law is the knowledge of sin" (Rom. 3:20). That which is true of this tenth commandment is true of the other nine. No man would have known Sabbath-breaking except the law had said, "The seventh day is the Sabbath of the Lord thy God; in it thou shalt not do any work" (Ex. 20:10). And he who does not know the fruits of Sabbath-breaking in his own life, will not know the fruits of Sabbath-breaking in the teaching of the workers of wonders.

He who would know the fruits of the false, must himself be delivered from the false, and he who would know the fruit of the true, must have the truth written upon his heart by the "Spirit of truth." He cannot and need not trust to the judgment and experience of another. "After those days, saith the Lord, I will put my law in their inward parts, and write it in their hearts. . . . And they shall teach no more every man his neighbor, and every man his brother, saying, Know the Lord; for they shall all know me, from the least of them unto the greatest of them, saith the Lord" (Jer. 31:33, 34). They who are delivered from delusion will be "those who by reason of use have their senses exercised to discern both good and evil" (Heb. 5:14).

Now of the things we have written, reader, this is the sum: You will not be deceived by the devil by "those miracles which he had power to do" if you do not grieve away the Spirit, which is sent to you to "guide you into all truth," by rejecting the truth to which the Spirit guides you. And you will not escape the deceiving power of the "great signs and wonders" unless you yourself are perfectly acquainted with the fruits of the Spirit, yourself "being fruitful in every good work" (Col. 1:10) because you are yourself "filled with the Spirit." "Receive ye the Holy Ghost."

CHAPTER FORTY-THREE

HOW APOSTLES AND PROPHETS ARE CHOSEN

Because the gifts of the Spirit should be present in the church; because there should be apostles, prophets, evangelists, pastors, and teachers, it does not follow that it is the work of the church to *elect* them. There are those who, finding that the perfect, scriptural church has all these offices, have gone about to make a perfect church by electing men to fill these positions. Having done this, they talk much of the apostolic church, and point to their apostles, prophets, and evangelists, and challenge others to point out these gifts in their churches. While it is true that all these gifts do not appear in the church, yet it is sadder to see these positions filled by men who were placed there by the vote of their brethren, not because they were anointed by the Holy Ghost to exercise the gifts, but because it is seen that these offices exist in the perfect church, and because it is thought to be the duty of the church to keep all these offices filled.

But apostles, prophets, evangelists, pastors, and teachers, with all the other instrumentalities through whom the gifts of the Spirit are manifested in the church, are chosen, qualified, and sent of God to the church to be received or rejected by the church. The office does not qualify the man; the man must first be qualified for the office.

Israel never elected her true prophets. She did choose some prophets, but they were all false prophets. God elected all the true prophets and sent them to warn Israel; and it was left to Israel to receive or reject them, but not to elect them.

"And the Lord God of their fathers *sent* to them by his messengers, rising up betimes, and sending; because he had compassion on his people, and on his dwelling place; but they mocked the messengers of God, and despised his words, and misused his prophets" (II Chron. 36:15, 16).

"Behold, I *send* unto you prophets, and wise men, and scribes" (Matt. 23:34).

"And *God* hath *set* some in the church, first apostles, secondarily prophets, thirdly teachers, after that miracles, then gifts of healings, helps, governments, diversities of tongues" (I Cor. 12:28).

Apostles and prophets made by the church would serve those who made them, as the false prophets which backslidden Israel made, served her. But all the human agents through whom God manifests the gifts of the Spirit, are chosen and sent of God to serve Him, not the people.

Paul is an illustration of the relative relation which the Lord and the people sustain to those who exercise the gifts of the Spirit. The Lord chose Paul to exercise the gift of an apostle. It was left with the church to recognize that God had set Paul in their midst as an apostle. It was several years before the church recognized Paul's apostleship, but all this time he was recognized by the Lord as an apostle. The story of Paul's experience in being recognized by the church as an apostle is found in the first and second chapters of Galatians, a portion of which reads thus:

"And when James, Cephas, and John, who seemed to be pillars, perceived the grace that was given unto me, they gave to me and Barnabas the right hands of fellowship; that we should go unto the heathen, and they unto the circumcision" (Gal. 2:9).

All this teaches that God elects men to exercise the gifts of the Spirit in the church, and that it is left with the church to recognize, or reject, the grace which has been given them. It therefore follows that if some of the gifts are lacking in the church, it is not the work of the church to go about to fill the vacant offices by electing men to them. The work of the church is to put away sin and seek the Lord to manifest the missing gifts, and to ask for grace to discern them when He does manifest them.

It is better by far to have the seats empty than to have them occupied by men whom God has not seated. For when the seats are filled, the church is satisfied and will not humble herself and seek God for the missing gifts. And again, when the seats are filled by the will of men, those thus seated are sure to fight those whom God sends to occupy the seats.

While it is humbling to see empty seats where the gifts of the Spirit should appear, yet it is more humbling to see them filled by those who have a form of godliness without the power. The church which leaves the seats empty, and waits and prays to God to fill them, shows more spiritual discernment, and is far more apostolic, than one which fills these seats with men whom God has not qualified and sent.

CHAPTER FORTY-FOUR

WHAT IS THE OUTLOOK?

Since we must have a church with apostolic purity
before we can have a church with apostolic power, what
is the outlook for such a church? Will it ever appear?
Will it not require many years to cleanse the church
if, indeed, it will ever be done? How and by whom will
it be accomplished?

The heat of the furnace was like the sevenfold
heated furnace of Nebuchadnezzar. Through the great
airshafts there came a mighty, rushing wind, and it
fanned the flames into a fury. Tongues of fire darted
through the great mass of limestone and coke and
iron ore. Men were unloading into this fiery furnace
a kind of rock in which they said were gold and silver.
I picked up a glittering piece of ore and thought I saw
gold, but the guide said it was pyrites of iron. "It
is not all gold that glitters."

Then we went below to the base of the furnace.
The mighty, rushing wind had fanned the furnace
fires to smelting heat, and the coke, and the limestone,
and the iron, and the quartz, and the copper, and the
gold, and the silver, were all a molten sea.

And then I saw a wonder. There were two outlets on different sides of the furnace. From the larger one there flowed a great fiery stream. They told me it was the limestone, coke, iron, and quartz. From the smaller opening there ran forth a little stream of precious metals. Substances which had dwelt together for ages in the bosom of the earth, now ran away from each other with a haste that seemed to voice a mutual hate.

The little particles of precious metals that had been scattered through the ore and imprisoned in their rocky cells for centuries, now ran together and embraced each other with a speed and sparkle that looked akin to joy. This was the miner's harvest time.

As I thought upon the fiery furnace, which men call a smelter, and saw how easily they could separate the precious metal from the base, I remembered the precious children of God who are mingled with the base in the church and the world, and I sighed and said, "Oh, for a Divine Smelter!"

Then the Lord spake through His Word and said: "He shall baptize you with the Holy Ghost, and with fire; whose fan is in his hand, and he will throughly purge his floor, and gather his wheat into the garner; but he will burn up the chaff with unquenchable fire" (Matt. 3:11, 12). "Behold, I will send my messenger, and he shall prepare the way before me; and the Lord, whom ye seek, shall suddenly come to his temple, even the messenger of the covenant, whom ye delight in; behold, he shall come, saith the Lord of hosts. But who may abide the day of his coming? and who shall stand when he appeareth? for he is like a refiner's fire, and like fullers' soap; and he shall sit as a refiner and purifier of silver; and he shall purify the sons of Levi, and purge them as gold and silver, that they may offer unto the Lord an offering in righteousness" (Mal. 3:1–3).

The Holy Spirit is the Lord's smelting furnace. In it He separates the precious from the base. It purifies the gold and causes it to shine forth in all its heavenly luster, while it burns up the hypocritical glitter of the dross.

These furnace fires were kindled on the day of Pentecost when the mighty, rushing wind came to the "upper room," followed by the tongues of fire. Into this furnace there was cast the new-born church of Jesus Christ; but the dross had already been burned out, and the pure gold only shone the brighter amid the glare of the furnace fires. Then the Lord cast into the furnace the Jewish church, with its priesthood of pomp and pride, and then the whole Gentile world, with its tinsel and show. The mighty, rushing wind continued to blow, and the tongues of fire continued to burn, until the whole was a molten sea and the pure was separated from the vile, and under God's furnace fires the world was separated into but two elements: the precious and the base, martyrs and murderers.

This was God's early harvest-time, the firstfruits of the great last-day harvest. Oh, that the church had kept the furnace fires burning at smelting heat! But they were allowed to cool, and the precious and the base are today mingled in a mighty mass, awaiting the furnace fires which the Holy Ghost has again begun to fan to smelting heat.

Yes, it has *begun*. There is a movement toward the "upper room" among those who sigh and cry for all the abominations which are done in the midst of a backslidden church. There is a crying to God for "power from on high." There is a baptizing with the Holy Ghost. There is a running together of the "free gold," of those in whom the purging fires are burning, and from whose faces the Lord has wiped the wrinkling dross of sin. A nucleus is forming, like the nucleus that formed on the day of Pentecost. And soon again the whole church and the world will be in the baptistry of God's burning presence, in His latter-day furnace. Forth from its purifying flames will come the church of God, though only a remnant, without spot or wrinkle or any such thing.

I said the furnace fires had begun to burn. How do I know? Because I have felt the flame. Many men and women in the church to which I belong have cast themselves into the purifying furnace of God's Holy Spirit; and I have seen the great Refiner of silver wipe from their darkened faces the wrinkling dross of sin, and leave them shining with holy consecration. And this holy shining is throwing its searchlight upon those who are base and vile within the church. They cannot endure the glory, for the separating time has come because the Holy Ghost has come; "but who may abide the day of his coming?"

These two elements cannot long dwell together under the smelting power of the Holy Spirit. They do not belong together. One is the tried gold of faith; the other is base unbelief. And under the baptismal fire of the Holy Spirit, the man of faith will flee from the Babylon of unbelief, even as Lot fled from Sodom.

It was after the service. For ten days we had been in the purifying furnace. We had just prayed for the Holy Spirit for witnessing power. I shook hands with a minister and his wife, members of another denomination, who were present at the service. After expressing their sympathy with the work of the meeting, the wife asked with earnest frankness, "Do your people *live* this?" And again, "Are all your people receiving the Spirit thus?" When told that the work was going from conference to conference like a prairie fire, she answered, "I am so glad." Then she explained her joy: "In yonder church there is a faithful mother in Israel who protests against the worldward drift of her church. She refuses to share its pride and worldly pleasure. God is blessing her with His Spirit. Over in that other church there is a man of God. He is a living rebuke to his backslidden church, and God is blessing him with His Spirit. But there ought to be a *whole church* somewhere baptized with the Holy Ghost."

These words burned into my soul. True, there ought to be a *whole church* somewhere baptized with the Holy Ghost. This is one of many heart-cries from the imprisoned gold. And God will answer that cry. There will be a baptized church; yes, a *visible* church. The Lord left a *visible*, baptized church when He went away. He declared that the gates of hell should not prevail against that church, and they will not.

When He returns, He will find a visible church baptized with the Holy Ghost, without spot or wrinkle, awaiting His return.

There is an ever-increasing procession leading towards the "upper room." Reader, are you one of them? And just as the precious metals obeyed the divine law and left the lighter, baser metal and ran together, so the gold that is mixed with the base in the church and the world, under the smelting heat of the Holy Ghost, will yet hear the voice of God from heaven, saying: "Babylon the great is fallen, is fallen. . . . Come out of her, my people, that ye be not partakers of her sins, and that ye receive not of her plagues. For her sins have reached unto heaven, and God hath remembered her iniquities."

The furnace fires have begun to burn. God's latter-day harvest will soon be gathered. Reader, are you in the furnace? Are you being baptized with the Holy Ghost? Are you willing to be cleansed? If so, get into the furnace. "Receive ye the Holy Ghost."